METRO ✡ JEWISH RESOURCES

JEWISH EVANGELISM TRAINING MANUAL

AN ANTHOLOGY OF KEY TOPICS
FOR JEWISH OUTREACH

All rights reserved. This book or parts thereof may not be reproduced in any form, stored in any retrieval system, or transmitted in any form by any means – electronic, mechanical, photocopy, recording, or otherwise – without prior written permission of Metro Jewish Resources, except as provided by United States of America copyright law. For permission requests, contact MJR at Metro Jewish Resources, PO Box 3777, Wayne, NJ 07074.

Dear Pastor, Ministry Leader and Mission's Directors:

The chapters compiled for this book were selected by Metro Jewish Resources. As with most anthologies, the chapters offer a wide range of subjects, of different perspectives from the personal, experiential, and others in Jewish ministry.

The first goal of this book is to help clarify the form for Jewish ministry of what is called, Jewish Evangelism, and to show how the rush toward understanding the history and culture of the Chosen People given the last days that we are in, and the mandate upon the church to reach the Jew is of utmost import throughout this manual.

The second goal is to suggest that the process towards understanding and formulating a Jewish outreach ministry, must be brought to the fore of any outreach effort to prevent the historical injury to the Gospel to the Jew. This becomes clear throughout the chapters that have been selected.

The third goal is to equip church leadership and laity. We seek to seed the local Church community to be an effective bridge to their local Jewish community while building upon commonalities and sensitivities that draw Jewish people to their Jewish Messiah. Our hope is that this first Jewish Training manual become a rich source of insight to the many challenges that face Jewish ministry, too a valuable reference for years to come. Endorsed by major ministries, much team work came together to make this complete. For my wife Bonnie and I it represents over 20 years of Jewish ministry. We are grateful to the Lord for what He has done in making this training manual possible.

ACKNOWLEDGMENTS

I wish to thank my wife and partner Bonnie for her grace and patience over the last four months during the tireless effort to reach the completion date that was needed for this work. Her encouragement and shared vision enabled my efforts to go forth. My daughter Heather with her experience in writing spent many hours in developing and editing this manual that was greatly appreciated.

I want to give recognition to the partnership of Sal Miliziano, our Executive Vice President for his support, shared vision and encouragement. To the wonderful leadership of Malcolm Burleigh, and the continued support of Qene Jeffers, and the entire US Missions team has been invaluable. Without their partnership, friendship and kingdom purpose for MJR, we could not have reached these important milestones as this manual, and other upcoming resource material.

It has also been a privilege and joy to collaborate with Rabbi Myron Slobin on the development of this work. His sacrificial work and time to bring this product to its completion are deeply appreciated and valued. He has been a great aid and contributor. Jodi and Kent Smith's editing work along with Marcie and Joe Kenny provided an invaluable service to ensure that this manual reaches the point of completion. Their efforts are greatly appreciated and valued.

MORE INDIVIDUALS DESERVE RECOGNITION

Thank you, Pastor Carl Colletti, New Jersey District Superintendent, and Pastor Rich Leksell, New Jersey District Missions Director, for opening the first resource office for Jewish Ministry, and staying the course with me. I also appreciate Dr. Duane Durst, New York District Superintendent and David Nuzzolo for their cooperation and partnership in the most important Jewish epicenter outside of Israel. To Pastor Manny Alverez, Spanish Eastern District Superintendent, and Ramon Hernandez, Spanish Eastern District Missions Director, as well Pastor Alberto Torres for your faith and support in this work. I say thank you for your support and constant encouragement to the establishment of this office.

ENDORSEMENTS

I have known Felix Halpern for many years. We have dialogued together, and he has drunk deeply of the Bible and in interaction with the Messianic Jewish Movement. I see much of my writings reflected in Felix's writing. I hope that is true. I think Felix has studied well and has produced a very valuable manual. I have been in the Messianic Jewish stream for over 44 years and am so glad for the progress shown by this manual.

- Dr. Daniel Juster, Tikkun International

In a world where we are witnessing a rising tide of anti-Semitism as well as anti-Israel sentiment, I am grateful to God for this new training manual. Jewish people are open to the gospel right now and especially this millennial generation of Jews. How very important it is then for God's people to be educated and equipped to show His love to the Jewish people and to learn to be effective in sharing that love in Jesus with them. Many blessings to brother Halpern and the MJR as they use this manual to pursue that vital ministry.

- David Brickner, Executive Director/ Jews for Jesus

Felix Halpern has written an excellent workbook for training Christians in the work of Jewish evangelism. His effort provides 130 pages plus of superb theological, historical and practical information. The practical sections are very much needed and are written and presented in an easy to follow format that should enable Christians to utilize this information in sharing a clear and sensitive Jewish Gospel to their Jewish friends, neighbors, and relatives. It is no wonder that Felix has created such an effective training tool for today's church! He is a Jewish believer himself with many years of ministry experience among his fellow Jewish people as both an evangelist and Rabbi of a Messianic Congregation. We hope this manual will be used by thousands of Assembly of God churches and that an army of Jewish evangelists would be raised up in these last days.

We also expect that many other Christian groups will take good advantage of this excellent tool by using it for home Bible studies, small groups, and training services at the church. Finally, Felix goes to great lengths to show that the role of the Jewish people and the land of Israel is not merely the initiative of modern day's politicians or leaders, or even transformative historical events like the Holocaust. Felix has given a rightful place to these significant events in the Jewish story but more importantly had developed a kingdom themed theology showing the role of the Jew throughout history in the kingdom of God and in preparing the world for the coming of our great King and Messiah, *Yeshua Hamashicah*. Chosen People Ministries applauds Felix on a job well done and for the creation of a new tool for training Christians to reach Jewish people for the Lord Jesus.

- Dr. Mitch Glaser, Director of Chosen People Ministries

In his passion for the "Salvation of All Israel," Felix Halpern has created a study guide and seminar manual that is sure to equip the Christian Children of Abraham on how to reach out and touch our Jewish families and friends with the Good News of *Yeshua*, Israel's Only Hope. In the bosom of every Born-Again, the Spirit-filled believer is the deep-seated conviction that God still eagerly wants every Jewish person to worship Him in Spirit and Truth. That purity of spiritual worship comes with true faith in the Jewish Messiah *Yeshua*.

Felix Halpern's special passion for reaching Jewish Americans for Messiah Yeshua is critical to reaching the massive Jewish populations of New York, New Jersey and beyond. Just as the Scriptures make transparently clear "All Israel's" ongoing strategic role in global redemption, so resoundingly clear-cut is it that the **Christian proclamation** and **exhibition of *Yeshua*** is the catalyst for Israel's salvation (Romans. 11). May Felix Halpern's effective manual result in bringing into the Kingdom of God Jewish elderly, Jewish students, Jewish professionals, Jewish neighbors, indeed "All Israel" so that Jewish communities everywhere will honor Yeshua as King of Kings.

- Ray Gannon, Ph.D., National Jewish Field Representative

TABLE OF CONTENTS

Introduction 12

Section I Topics 15
Demographics 16-20
Messianic Leader Michael Rudolph 21-22

Section II Topics 24
What Are Your Expectations 25
General Principles 26
Common Questions That Jewish People Ask 27
Four Meaningful Questions 28
Break Out Session 29

Section III Topics 31
Building with The Holy Spirit 32
Prayer & Power & Signs and Wonders Evangelism 33-37
The Working Gears of Jewish Evangelism 38-39

Section IV Topics 40
New Testament: Building Effective Jewish Ministry 41-43
Old Testament: Building Effective Jewish Ministry 44
Words from Dr. Mitch Glaser 45
Memory Block Set I: Messiah's Birth 46

Section V Topics 47
Historical Acts of Anti-Semitism I: 48-49
More Voices of Jewish Hate 50-52
Questions to Reflect Upon 53-54
Memory Block Scriptures 55

Historical Acts of Antisemitism II; 56
Six "C" Words That Became a Sword of Offense..............................56-57
Replacement Terms for Effective Jewish Outreach..............................56
Historical Acts of Anti-Semitism III..58-64
American Anti-Semitism... 64
Thomas Jefferson..66
Henry Ford..67
Yale and Harvard..67

Section VI Topics..71

Seven Questions of Judaism..74-80
Words from Rabbi Slobin..81
Memory Block..83
Jewish Objections to Christian Messianic Claims....................84
Jewish History..86
Why Jewish People Do Not Believe in Jesus...........................87-90
- Culture.
- Pluralism.
- Monotheism
- Dualism

Section VII Topics..91

Understanding Jewish Eschatology, History, Culture, Theology.........................92
Supplemental Study: Nine Sects of Judaism...101

Section VIII Topics...106

Jewish Election and the Kingdom..107-109
Kingdom Study Outline I..110-114
Kingdom Study Outline II...115-117

The Future Age……………………………………………………………..119-120

The Purpose of the Kingdom ……………………………………………………….117

Memory Block……………………………………………………………,……..121

Section IX Topics……………………………………………………..…..124

Israel: Whose Land Is It?……………………………………………………….125

Israel's Visionary………………………………………………………………126

Oppositionists / Assimilationists……………………………………...……..127

The Promised Land……………………………………………………………...128

Israel Today……………………………………………………………….129-130

Whose Land Is It Anyway? Part II…………………………………………132-135

Section X Topics……………………………………………………………139

Why Israel Will Endure Forever "Twelve Distinctions of Israel"………….140-142

The Twelve Distinctions of Israel Explained…………………………………143-152

Section XI Topics……………………………………………………………154

Applying What We Have Learned……………………………………..155-159

Jewishness of Messiah…………………………………………………..159-166

Indisputable Facts of the Messiah……………………………………………167-164

Section XII Topics…………………………………………………….175

Praying with a Jewish Person……………………………………………….. 176

A word from Dr. Mitch Glaser……………………………………………178-184

Appendix I: The Kingdom…………………………………………………..184

Appendix II: Wife of Jehovah Passages...192

Appendix III: More Blessings to The Gentiles...195

Appendix IV: Quick References and Prophecies…………………………….197

SYMBOLS USED IN MANUAL

	Information on Jewish demographics		For group study and discussion.
	Important key points from a particular section.		Important ministry of the Holy Spirit.
	Important points to target ones focus.		Old Testament Prophecies.
	Place for personal reflection.		Study questions.
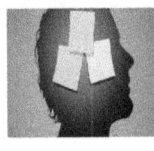	Important memory blocks of Scripture.		Anti-Jewish rulings of the Catholic Church.

It is critically important to recognize that the course we are on given our times, The Good News to the Jewish People coupled with an historical and cultural awareness, brings an understanding of God's Chosen People, and conveys God's love. There is surely no more important consequence of this on Jewish outreach than learning, training, and equipping for the Jewish harvest.

INTRODUCTION

"For the church to evangelize the world without thinking of the Jews is like a bird trying to fly with one broken wing."

Franz Delitzsch, (1813-1890)

Metro Jewish Resources has been created at a time in world events that suggests God is drawing His people to Him in very profound ways. The end times seem to be in season, and this ministry sees itself as having been assigned by God through the National Assemblies of God. Metro Jewish Resources (MJR) is playing a significant role in increasing the awareness of His reality that must be a part of the revival, restoration, and reconciliation between God and all of His children. Given this, Jewish evangelism is crucial, and preparing the Church to be an effective witness to the Jewish people. This is the goal and purpose of MJR.

As this denomination represents a very large body of believers and spiritual leaders, increasing this awareness of effective Jewish ministry through the National AG is a great opportunity that demands a national response. MJR is called to launch in the New York/ New Jersey Metro Region which contains the second largest Jewish population outside of Israel; approximately 3 million Jewish people reside in the greater Metropolitan area, close to 6 million nationally (see chart.) Today a growing interest is found in reaching the Jewish people with the Gospel of our Messiah. It is basically a measure of outreach that God has initiated both in the heart of the Gentile Christian body and an open heart in the Jewish people. Responsively, our churches must learn to articulate principles of New Covenant faith in a Jewish-friendly manner. Modalities for Jewish evangelism must present Christianity in a Jewish context, or at a minimum an understanding of Jewish history, and the historical persecutions that came in the name of Christianity.

Similarly, it is our hearts desire for individuals and churches to discover the vast and endless sea of Jewish evangelism—to receive the heart for the Jew and yearn to be part of what God is doing today. But regardless of all our efforts, nothing can substitute our spirit-empowered life and witness, which can provoke the Jew to envy according to Romans 11:11, *"Again I ask: Did they stumble so as to fall beyond recovery? Not at all! Rather, because of their transgression, salvation has come to the Gentiles to make Israel envious."*

In this first Jewish Evangelism Manual, each section presents a piece of a puzzle that comprises the whole of Jewish ministry. They entail **Culture**, **History**, and **Jewish Theology**, including a collection of the most asked questions regarding Jewish belief and evangelism. We seek to put them together to form one picture and explore such topics as, Jewish *calling, election, and purpose*. This manual provides concise and comprehensive teaching that will equip any congregation or individual to begin sharing the truth of Messiah with Jewish people. One will discover important truths regarding God's heart for Israel, and the fact that Israel will never be destroyed due to its God-given prophetic purpose. Located throughout this manual are study questions and memory blocks containing key Messianic prophecies that are important to commit to memory for the serious individual seeking to reach out to the Jewish people.

When it comes to Jewish evangelism, we strive to put *Yeshua* back into a Jewish framework, so Jewish people can experience how natural and complete it is to accept Him. The fact is, for a Jewish person to accept *Yeshua* is the most Jewish decision that a Jewish person can make, and one that is two thousand years old. Sharing the truth of Messiah with the Jewish people is simply telling others about the salvation that we received. But when we are equipped to dialogue with Jewish people about their culture and history, our testimony can be framed in a context that engages them. Our goal is to raise up an evangelistic force within our Churches that have a Missions heart, and a Missions mind.

As noted, sharing Messiah with Jewish people is simply telling others about the salvation that we received. But with great interest today in Jewish roots and Jewish identity, the more our testimony can be framed in a Jewish context, the more effective our efforts will be. At the same time, this does not mean that Gentiles should work hard to be Jewish or appear to be Jewish to Jewish people. Honesty and integrity are foremost. Jewish people have a keen ability to detect insincerity. What is required is simple: a "Missionary heart" and a "Missions mind."

For instance: The indigenous principle, something foundational to any mission's work, means that we minister to people in the means, manner, and method that best communicates the gospel of Messiah **within the context of their culture** (1 Co. 9:19-23). Though we bring much of our own tradition and culture to any outreach endeavor, we are bound to waLuke within the boundaries outlined in God's Word; *"Love casts out all fear"* John 1:4-8) *"We must be all things to all people,"* (1 Corinthians 9:19-31) *"For the purpose of Gentile salvation is to provoke the Jew to* *envy,"* (Romans 11:11.) Therefore, cultural traditions must not be mistaken for *"thus says the Lord."* We **must be flexible**. This is why a missionary heart and mind is essential. A Missionary heart and mind prompt two simple questions: **Do you have a desire to learn of the Jews and their history? Do you have a heart to be sensitive to the Jews and lovingly engage them with a historical and cultural sensitivity?**

Many social stigmas are encountered when reaching Jewish people with *Yeshua* that Gentiles do not experience in other outreaches. Often when witnessed to, Jewish people think about the **Pope, Crusades**, **Inquisition**, **Pogroms**, the **Holocaust,** not to mention, acts of anti-Semitism that were made against the Jewish people by so-called Christians during this Christian era. This is further complicated by the fact that Rabbis have been feeding them false information for centuries regarding who Jesus is, and His relevance for the Jewish people. They teach that Jesus and the New Testament are all about betraying and hating the Jewish people. These stumbling blocks are not something that a simple pamphlet given on the street can properly address.

To bring the gospel to the Jewish people need not be intimidating. In fact, when prepared and trained correctly, it can be exciting and invigorating. It will challenge you, I assure you! Jewish people are inquisitive, analytical, and circumspect, yet they cling to their Jewish identity. The plain notion of a Jew believing in Jesus, the Jewish Messiah (*Yeshua*), challenges modern day Judaism to its core. In fact, the only belief that contradicts Jewish identity (which comes with an arsenal of arguments to refute it) is the belief in Jesus. The plain truth is that Jewish people are searching! More Jewish people are coming to faith, and the Church has been given a new heart for the Jewish people and Israel. God is moving profoundly in the hearts of Jewish people in these last days!

SECTION I

JEWISH DEMOGRAPHICS AND TRENDS

PRINCIPLES OF JEWISH EVANGELISM

DEMOGRAPHICS

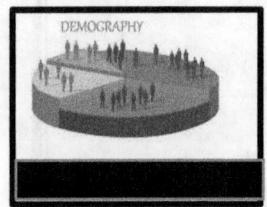

Regarding the United States, and according to the "World Jewish Counsel," it is home to the largest, or second-largest, Jewish population in the world, depending on sources cited and methods used. The American Jewish community boasts a wide range of Jewish cultural traditions encompassing the full spectrum of Jewish religious strands and traditions. About half of American Jews can be considered religious. There is a sprawling network of Jewish communities, organizations and institutions, and Jews often taken an active interest in public life and debate. Kosher food is widely available.

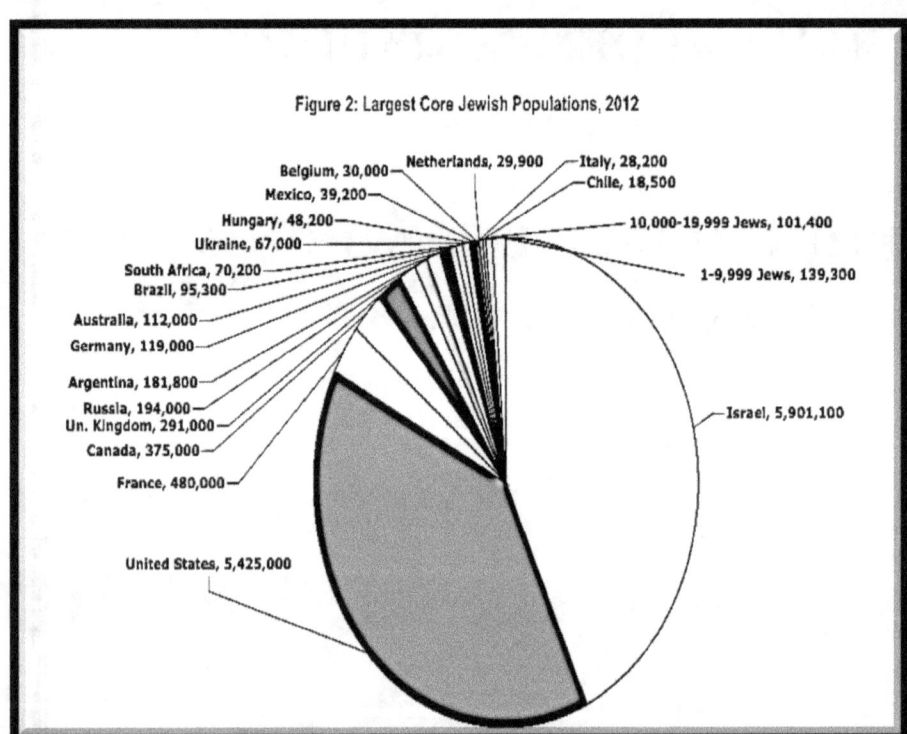

With between 5,300,000 and 7,000,000 million Jews, the United States is home to what is considered the largest Jewish population in the world outside of Israel, depending on the sources cited and methods used. The precise population figures vary depending on whether Jews are accounted for based on halachic considerations, or secular, political and ancestral identification factors. With its two million Jews, New York is the largest Jewish city in the world.

About half of American Jews are considered to be religious. A 2003 poll found that 16 percent of American Jews go to synagogue at least once a month, 42 percent go less frequently but at least once a year, and 42 percent attend services less than once a year. Among those who belong to a synagogue, 38 percent are members of Reform, 33 percent of Conservative, 22 percent of Orthodox, and 2 percent of Reconstructionist synagogues.

Jewish Americans are more likely to be atheist or agnostic than those belonging to other faith groups, especially in comparison with Protestants or Catholics. A poll found that while 79 percent of Americans believe in God, only 48 percent of Jewish Americans do. Jews play an active role in art, media, and entertainment. The proportion of Jewish university graduates is higher than that of the general population, and Jews hold many high positions in government, or are members of Congress. Many of the country's outstanding universities are headed by Jews, and all include a disproportionately large Jewish student population. Jewish cuisine (particularly the bagel) is widely enjoyed by non-Jews, and Jewish motifs are an integral part of American culture, constituting a distinct sub culture. Moreover, many Yiddish words have crept into the general idiom (e.g. chutzpa, schlep, schlemiel, yenta, meshuga, megilla). Certain Jewish communities form groups that preserve special customs and traditions. These include the Bukharan and Syrian Jews in Queens, NY; Russian Jews in Brighton Beach, Brooklyn, NY; and Iranian Jews in Los Angeles, CA. The United States – particularly Brooklyn – is also the home of many Chassidic groups.

The demographic survey of American Jewry published in 1991 was viewed by many as a redundant watershed. The dramatic revelations on the rate of intermarriage (more than 50 percent) and assimilation aroused a feeling of pessimism in the life of the community. The study, commissioned by the Council of Jewish Federations, estimated the 'core' Jewish population at 4.1 million (or 5.8 million based on local community counts). Only 3.5 million belonged to families in which both parents were Jews. In the last two to three decades, there has been a double movement of Jews away from the Northeast (and to some extent from the Midwest) to the South and West, and away from the big cities to the suburbs. These changes have served to dissolve established Jewish communities and have increased distances between Jewish centers, creating smaller and more dispersed communities. At the same time, many of the Jewish communities in smaller cities and towns are disappearing as younger Jews leave for the large urban areas."[1]

---

[1] http://www.worldjewishcongress.org/en/about/communities/US

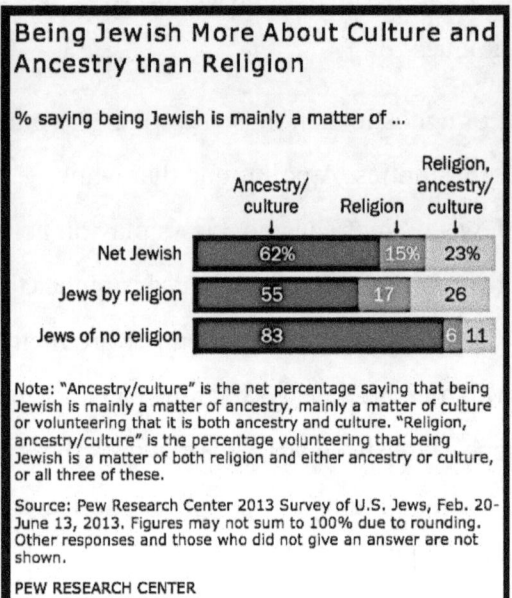
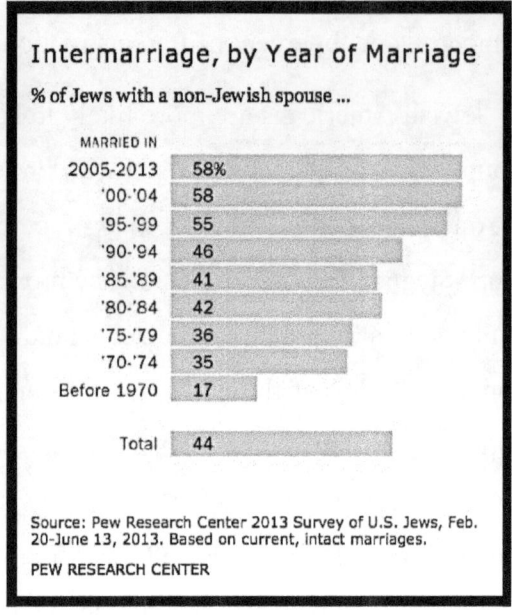
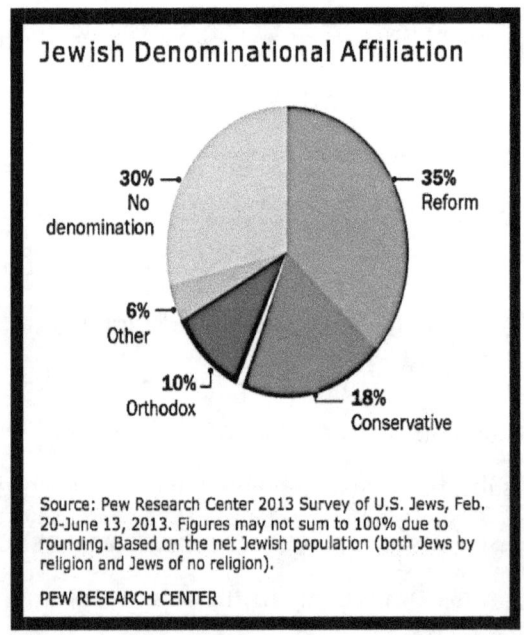

What is Compatible With Being Jewish?

Can a person be Jewish if he/she ...	Yes %	No %	DK %
... works on the Sabbath?	94	5	1=100
... is strongly critical of Israel?	89	9	2=100
... does not believe in God?	68	29	3=100
... believes Jesus was messiah?	34	60	6=100

Based on the net Jewish population.

Source: Pew Research Center 2013 Survey of U.S. Jews, Feb. 20-June 13, 2013.

PEW RESEARCH CENTER

Attachment, Attitudes About Israel

How emotionally attached are you to Israel?	NET Jewish %	Jews by religion %	Jews of no religion %
Very attached	30	36	12
Somewhat	39	40	33
Not very/Not at all	31	23	55
Don't know/Refused	1	1	*
	100	100	100
Been to Israel?			
Yes	43	49	23
No	57	51	77
Don't know	*	*	0
	100	100	100

Belief in God

	Believe in God or universal spirit, absolutely certain %	Believe, but less certain %	Do not believe %	Other/Don't know %
NET Jewish	34	38	23	5=100
Jews by religion	39	41	16	4=100
Jews of no religion	18	28	47	8=100

In What Way Do You Consider Yourself Jewish?

	Jewish back-ground %	Jewish affinity %
NET Background, family, ethnicity, ancestry, etc.	48	24
Raised Jewish/Jewish parent	22	2
Jewish grandparents	16	5
Ethnically/culturally Jewish	10	7
Jewish spouse	1	9
Have Jewish child/other relative	1	3
NET Religious reasons	20	59
Jesus was Jewish	8	31
Bible/scriptures	3	2
Jewish practices/holidays	3	6
Beliefs / values (general)	1	4
Messianic	*	3
Believe in God	1	1
NET Connection to or admiration for Jewish people	2	7
NET Other	3	11
Don't know	2	4
PARTIALLY JEWISH BY RELIGION	3	6
DO NOT CONSIDER SELF JEWISH	27	0

Source: Pew Research Center 2013 Survey of U.S. Jews, Feb. 20-June 13, 2013. QE1. Figures do not sum to 100% because multiple responses were permitted. Not all responses are shown.

PEW RESEARCH CENTER

About a third of Jews (32%) say they had a Christmas tree in their home last year, including 27% of Jews by religion and 51% of Jews of no religion. Erecting a Christmas tree is especially common among Jews who are married to non-Jews; 71% of this group says they put up a tree last year.

Compared with younger Jews, those 65 and older are somewhat less likely to have had a Christmas tree last year. And relatively few Orthodox Jews, including just 1% of Ultra-Orthodox Jews, say there was a Christmas tree in their home last year.

MESSIANIC LEADER
MICHAEL RUDOLPH

It is a privilege to incorporate different expert voices in this work. Michael Rudolph, an attorney, and long- time leader in the Messianic community, and key leader in Tikkun, is represented here from excerpts of a greater writing that was done on Jewish Evangelism. He writes the following:

"There are nine ways that most of us have been taught to minister Yeshua to unbelievers: The first, is giving testimony of our own experience in coming to faith. This is powerfully persuasive, and the Holy Spirit has been known to fall on the unbeliever while the testimony is being shared.

- The second method exposes the unbeliever to relevant Scriptures and seeks to answer his questions as to why the Scriptures are true, and the New Testament and Messiah Yeshua are Jewish. This method of evangelism is taught in some Messianic Jewish institutions of higher learning where it is known as "Jewish apologetics," and part of it is identifying Messianic prophecies in the *Tanakh*, and then demonstrating their fulfillment in the New Testament.

- The third method invites the unbeliever to a Messianic Jewish worship service in the hope that the Jewish environment, the message preached, or something else, will cause him to turn in his thinking and believe. That "something else" has to be the Holy Spirit who must be active in all of these methods for any of them to succeed.

- The fourth method presents Jews for Jesus's "Four Jewish Spiritual Laws." They are "oldies but goodies" – usually ministered from a small booklet or tract, and are so well thought out, simple, and effective, that I want to spend just a few minutes describing them.

    1. The first "Jewish Spiritual Law" is: "God loves you and has a wonderful plan for your life." The Scripture used to justify saying this is Jeremiah 31:2(3), which states:

2. The second "Jewish Spiritual Law" is: "Man is sinful and separated from God, and thus he cannot know and experience God's Love and Plan for his life." Explained another way: "Man is continually trying to have an abundant life through his own efforts – good deeds, ethical conduct, philosophy, etc." The Scripture used to justify saying this is Ecclesiastes 7:20, which reads:

3. The third "Jewish Spiritual Law" is: "The Messiah is God's only provision for man's sin. Through Him you can know God's Love and Plan for your life." The Scripture used to justify saying this is Leviticus 17:11, that says:

4. The fourth "Jewish Spiritual Law" is: "We must receive Messiah Yeshua as Savior and LORD by personal invitation." The Scripture used to justify saying this is Psalms 2:12, which states: Kiss his son, or he will be angry, and your way will lead to your destruction, for his wrath can flare up in a moment. Blessed are all who take refuge in him."

5. The fifth is inviting the unbeliever to a small group teaching or discussion.

6. The sixth is to nurture a friendship relationship with him and ministering Yeshua to him when the time is right.

7. The seventh, allow the way we conduct our life to be a witness of our faith.

8. The eight, find ways to serve the unbeliever's needs and those for whom he/she cares about.

9. The ninth, pray for the unbeliever's salvation.

All of these are good and effective if done at the direction of the Holy Spirit. Also, we are not to become discouraged if we do not see results. In my own case, for example, the Lord brought quite a few believers across my path before the Holy Spirit zapped me into the Kingdom while the man who was witnessing to me kept talking because he didn't even know what had happened.

- *We must employ education and training to become effective in one of the most challenging fields of evangelism. I greatly favor the following quote,* **"If you want to build a ship, don't drum up the men to gather wood, divide the work and give**

- ***orders. Instead, teach them to yearn for the vast and endless sea."*** – Antoine de Saint-Exupery

- *Jewish outreach involves understanding their **Culture**, **History**, and **Theology**.*

- *What is required is simple: a "Missionary heart" and a "Missions mind."*

- *Many social stigmas are encountered when reaching Jewish people with Yeshua that Gentiles do not experience in other outreaches. Often upon witnessing, Jewish people think about the **Pope, Crusades, Inquisition, Pogroms**, the **Holocaust**, not to mention, acts of anti-Semitism that were made against the Jewish people by so-called Christians during this Christian era.*

- *More Jewish people are coming to faith, and the Church has been given a new heart for the Jewish people and Israel. Therefore, God is moving profoundly in the hearts of Jewish people in these last days.*

- *The indigenous principle, something foundational to any mission's work, means that we minister to people in the means, manner, and method that best communicates the gospel of Messiah **within the context of their culture** (1 Corinthians. 9:19-23).*

- *Cultural traditions must not be mistaken for "thus says the Lord." We **must be flexible**. This is why a missionary heart and mind is essential. A Missionary heart and mind prompt two simple questions:*

- *Do you have a desire to learn of the Jew and their history? Do you have a heart to be sensitive to the Jew and lovingly engage them with a historical and cultural sensitivity?*

SECTION II

GENERAL PRINCIPLES

COMMON QUESTIONS JEWISH PEOPLE ASK

MEANINGFUL QUESTIONS

BREAK OUT SESSION

WHAT ARE YOUR EXPECTATIONS FROM THIS TRAINING?

This section begins to build a foundation for understanding the unique challenges facing Jewish evangelism. We begin with general principles, but of equal importance, register your expectations from this training time in the space provided at the end of this section. Often, our expectations may either be realistic or not, too being influenced by our own experiences with Jewish people, or even our theological orientations. Provided also at the end are 4 meaningful questions) to help identify our motivation and perspective. Then we have the chance to share with others in a "Break Our Session" to deepen our understanding and also prompt our own misconceptions.

Check below what best describes your knowledge of the Jewish people and the Jewish religion.

Adequate _____ Well Versed _____ No Understanding _____

Know key Scriptures pertaining to witnessing to Jewish people. *"Study to shew thyself approved unto God, a workman that needeth not to be ashamed, rightly dividing the word of truth." (2 Timothy 2:15)*

1. Do not be afraid or timid but be confident in God's Word. As Paul stated, it is the Jew first, and the Spirit of God will help us. (Romans 1:16) *"For I am not ashamed of the*

gospel because it is the power of God that brings salvation to everyone who believes: first to the Jew, then to the Gentile."

2. Be sensitive and don't let boldness overshadow the need for wisdom in speaking to Jewish people; look for insight into opportunities. (Matthew 10:16) *"I am sending you out like sheep among wolves. Therefore, be as shrewd as snakes and as innocent as doves."*

3. Resist being argumentative, rather show interest in hearing what the person is saying, always respond with kindness and understanding. Share compassionately and do not be overbearing (John 13:35) Never pass up an opportunity to share the Good News of Messiah with others. *"By this everyone will know that you are my disciples if you love one another."*

4. Anticipate Results! Just like a farmer knows the laws of the harvest and the process of producing a crop, witness to win: The soil is ready, God has given you the seed, and the seed is ready to take root. Many have had the seed already planted, and the Lord of the Harvest has been watering it, and it is ready to spring forth. When you are sharing with a Jewish person, you could be the one that leads them to their Messiah, and a harvest is experienced. (John 4:35) *"Don't you have a saying, 'It's still four months until harvest'? I tell you, open your eyes and look at the fields! They are ripe for harvest.' The fruit of the righteous is a tree of life, and the one who is wise saves lives." (Proverbs 11:30.)*

5. Using Messianic terminology that puts *Yeshua* back in His Jewish framework."

To the Jews I became a Jew, to win the Jews. To those under the law, I became like one under the law (though I myself am not under the law) so as to win those under the law. To those not having the law, I became like one not having the law (though I am not free from God's law but am under Christ's law), so as to win those not having the law. To the weak I became weak, to win the weak. I have become all things to all people so that by all possible means I might save some. I do all this for the sake of the gospel that I may share in its blessings (1 Corinthians 9:19-23.)

6. Always remain sensitive and loving and realizing the historical prejudices against the Messiah that were formed throughout Jewish history.

7. Be comfortable when confronted with specific questions that Jewish people ask; use those opportunities to become more effective in presenting the Gospel of Christ to the Jewish people.

COMMON JEWISH QUESTIONS

1. Why do all of my Jewish friends, family, and Rabbi reject Jesus as the Jewish Messiah?

2. What is the difference between the Christian Bible and Jewish Bible?

3. Why do most Jews reject Jesus as the Jewish Messiah?

4. How can someone else die for someone's sins?

5. Why do Christians believe in three Gods?

6. How is the New Testament a Jewish book?

7. If Jewish people are the chosen people, why have they been persecuted and subjected to so much anti-Semitism?

REVIEW THESE PASSAGES:

2 Timothy. 2:15:

Romans 1:16;

Matthew 10:16;

John13:35;

John 4:35;

Proverbs. 11:30;

4 MEANINGFUL QUESTIONS

- Do I have a genuine regard for the Jewish people rooted in a realistic, and scriptural understanding of who they are?

- Am I willing to commit myself to actively reaching out to Jewish friends and neighbors with the message of Messiah *Yeshua*? Am I willing to put up with the rejection which may result?

- Am I willing to view myself as a servant of the Lord in my local church for the sake of the well-being of his people Israel?

- Am I willing to study the history, culture, and current life experience of the Jewish people, so I can gain an ever-deepening sense of the Jewish people as they "are," and not just as they are "supposed to be" according to some idealized understanding?

First exercise: Describe your fears and apprehensions in sharing the Gospel with Jewish people.

Second exercise: What do you perceive as your greatest obstacle to reaching Jewish people?

Third exercise: Can you relate an experience that you had in witnessing to a Jewish person.

Fourth exercise: List in one-word answers how you describe the Jewish people? It is important, to be honest and transparent.

Fifth exercise: Explain your heart for Jewish ministry and why it is important to reach the Jewish People. If able, use the Romans road of evangelism (Romans 1:1, 11: 11,16, 15:26.)

NOTES:

SECTION III

BUILDING WITH THE HOLY SPIRIT

BUILDING A JEWISH MINISTY

PRAYER & POWER EVANGELISM

WORKING GEARS OF JEWISH EVANGELISM

> TO UNDERSTAND THAT THE POWER OF THE HOLY SPIRIT IS VITAL TO JEWISH ENGAGEMENT OF THE GOSPEL, REACHING JEWISH PEOPLE CANNOT BE DONE WITH INTELLECTUAL REASONING. IT MUST BE ACCOMPLISHED WITH THE DIVINE PARTNERSHIP WITH THE HOLY SPIRIT. FOR THIS REASON, WE DISCUSS POWER EVANGELISM, PROPHETIC EVANGELISM AND SIGNS AND WONDERS DEMONSTRATIONS. WITH THIS IN HAND, IT FORMULATES A 3-STEP PROCESS WHILE OFFERING 5 KEY POINTS OF JEWISH OUTREACH BELOW.

"There are many things that are helpful in Jewish evangelism. Learning how to speak into Jewish culture is important. Presenting the Gospel in a Jewish way is important. Knowing how to present apologetics in a Jewish way on fulfilled prophecy and the resurrection of Jesus is important. But after 44 years plus of Jewish ministry, I want to say that the most important thing of all is the power of the Holy Spirit and knowing the voice of the Spirit in the interaction with others. Yes, friendship is a good thing in evangelism, but the power of the Spirit is the great equalizer and can make us adequate for all situations to which God call us."

- **Dr. Daniel Juster, (Director of Tikkun International)**

With all the preparation, study and organization, there is no substitute for Spirit-Empowered Evangelism when it comes to the Jewish people. Certainly, this can be said of all evangelism, but Jewish people remain a people that look for a sign. They have a proclivity for the supernatural. *"For Jews request a sign, and Greeks seek after wisdom"* (1 Corinthians 1:22-25).

Two thousand years after *Yeshua's* advent, Jews still have a sensitivity to God's presence and a deep interest in the supernatural. With this in mind, we encourage the following to be a central piece of any Jewish evangelism.

As noted by Dr. Juster, who is considered both a pioneer and a grandfather of the Messianic movement, notes that the *"power of the Spirit is the great equalizer."* As Pentecostals, the induement of power from the Spirit (Luke 24:29; Joel 2:27-28) and subsequent Gifts. (1 Corinthians. 12 and 14) often holds the "provocative charge" to dead and lifeless bones to this day. "Should the bones live" which can only come from our Lord's sacrifice, the power of the Spirit will be our companion, he will prompt us and provoke us. Only by the Spirit can the veil over the eyes of the Jewish people be removed! (2 Corinthians 3:14) One thing that I have discovered in over 20 years of Messianic ministry: one cannot win Jewish people to faith through intellect, or reason, but only through a tangible demonstration of God's power.

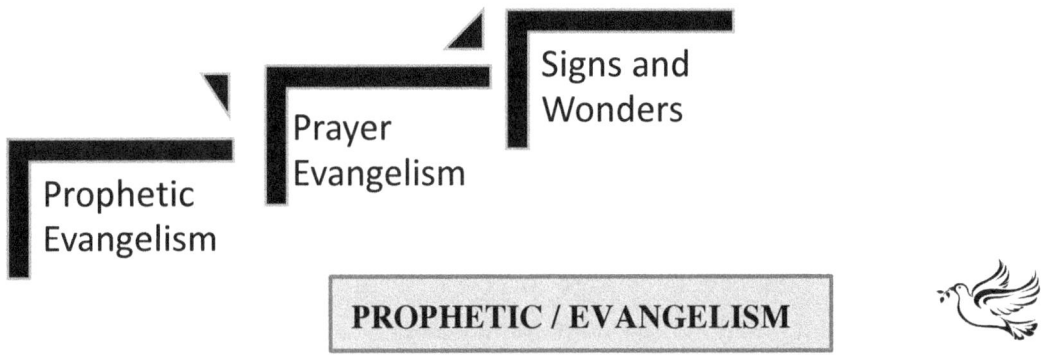

PROPHETIC / EVANGELISM

I Corinthians 14:1-3, Paul tells us to *"pursue love, yet earnestly desire spiritual gifts, but especially that you may prophesy."* Translated literally, it means what we should "lust" after prophecy. But why is prophecy so important that we should pursue it?

1. 1. Prophecy is the power of God in your life flowing through the Holy Spirit.
2. 2. This gift or unction of the Spirit can often come when the Spirit through a human agent utters what man cannot know. Only the recipient and God have a knowledge

PRAYER / EVANGELISM

Sometimes the most valuable thing we can do for a person is to pray for them. Actually, prayer is always the most significant, vital, imperative, essential, critical, crucial…take your pick. The one thing prayer never is, is a waste. We like to walk a fine line when we talk about what we are doing in someone's life and then make sure to add statements like: "But, of course prayer is the most important thing, I'm just saying ...." When we pray, we offer sacrifice to God. We are a priestly people, and the priesthood is all about offering sacrifice to God. We offer our time and mental and emotional investment to God in prayer, so he can do with it as he pleases. If we pray for others, we can help to merit for them graces for courage to turn to God for atonement for their sins, and God's help to see how He is revealing Himself to the Jewish people.

1. Ask God to open their spiritual eyes (2 Corinthians 4:4).
2. Ask God to give them ears to hear (Matthew 13:15).
3. Ask God to give them faith to believe Acts 20:21).
4. Ask God to give them the will to respond (Romans 10:9).
5. Ask God to send people into their lives to witness to them (Matthew 9:38).
6. Ask God for ways to build caring relationships ((Colossians 3:12-13).
7. Also (Eph. 2:8-9; Phil. 1:29).
8. Ask God for opportunities to witness (Colossians. 4:3).
9. Ask God for a boldness to witness (Acts 4:29).
10. Ask God for an opportunity to invite them to a Sabbath service or a Bible study (Luke 14:23).
11. Ask God to set them free from the Rabbinic laws and traditions of Judaism (2 Timothy. 2:25-26).

SIGNS AND WONDERS EVANGELISM

We are to preach the Gospel not just with words, but also with power. Paul wrote: "Our gospel came to you not simply with words but also with power, with the Holy Spirit and deep conviction" (1 Thessalonians 1:5). God's message is not dependent on the rhetoric, and skills of men, He empowers our witness through His Spirit. And what does that power mean? It means signs and wonders—Let's believe it again!

I will not venture to speak of anything except what Yeshua has accomplished through me in leading the Gentiles to obey God by what I have said and done— by the power of signs and wonders, through the power of the Spirit of God. So, from Jerusalem all the way around to Illyricum, I have fully proclaimed the gospel of Christ (Rom 15:18-19).T

1. **WAIT ON THE LORD**: Wait on the Lord and be sensitive to the Holy Spirit. Prophecy is from the power of God through the Holy Spirit. This gift or unction of the Spirit is often manifested when God, through a human agent, God speaks forth what only the recipient and God have a knowledge of.

2. **PRAY FOR UNDERSTANDING:** For understanding and a word from the Lord before any witnessing to Jewish people.

3. **STUDY PROPHECY:** *"Study to shew thyself approved unto God, a workman that needeth not to be ashamed, rightly dividing the word of truth."* (2 Tim. 2:15) Since Jewish people are highly curious of the end times, especially given the tumultuous times that we in, and an increase of anti-Semitism, individuals

well versed in Biblical prophecy are a powerful tool in presenting the Gospel to the Jewish people.

4. **BE BOLD AND CONFIDENT IN GOD:** As we have the Word of God, remember, it is the true source of Truth. Acts 28:31 says that we should be proclaiming the kingdom of God and teaching about the Lord Jesus Christ with all boldness and without hindrance. Also, *"In him and through faith in him we may approach God with freedom and confidence."* (Eph. 3:12)

5. **DON'T FEEL THE NEED TO SHARE SOMETHING WHEN YOU HAVD NOTHING TO SAY:** In Jewish evangelism, it is best to follow your discernment and leading of the Holy Spirit rather than speaking words that may do more injury to your witness. Wait on the Lord as only He knows exactly what each person needs.

6. **PRAY FOR THE SICK AND EXPEXCT A MIRACLE!** Ask the Lord of the harvest to manifest Kingdom Power through your witness to Jewish people.

PRAYER & POWER EVANGELISM

When it comes to Jewish ministry, Jewish people love to receive prayer because they confront life's challenges as any other people group. Secondly, Jewish people are not taught that they can have a personal relationship with God, nor speak to God as a man speaks to a man (Exodus 33:11.) Hence, rarely in my life of ministry to the Jewish people have I experienced a Jewish person refuse prayer. This remains a tremendous door into a Jewish person's life. **We stress that when one is at a loss for any words to share, request for prayer is always a powerful starting point in engaging Jewish people.*

> As we believe that God is the same yesterday today and forever, His power is the same today to open blind eyes, unstop deaf ears, heal diseases and reverse every curse and infirmity in the human body. Miracles still occur on a daily basis. Not the least is when someone comes to faith when their spiritual eyes are opened, and immediately they are able to see what they previously could not. Today, Jewish people are searching for Truth with a new fervor. When you pray for them, expect the Holy Spirit to touch them profoundly; act and expect in order to receive.

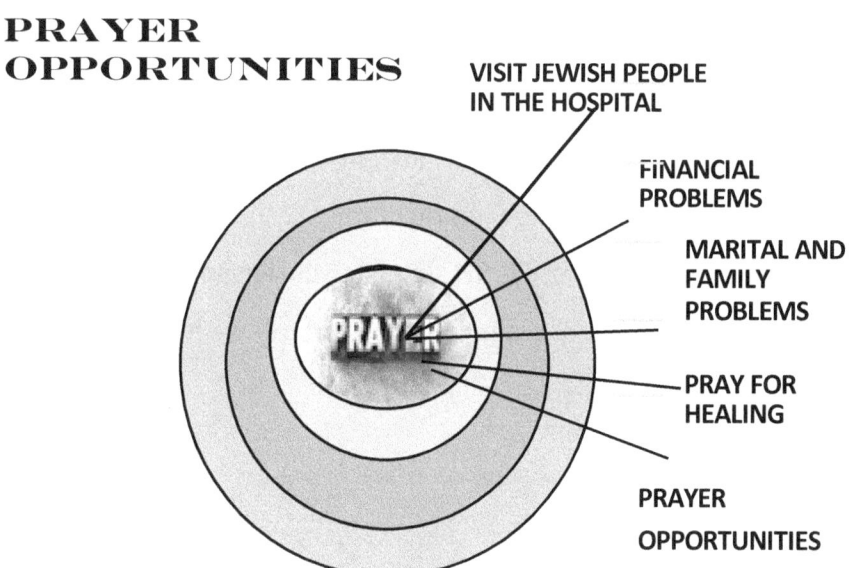

POWER EVANGELISM:

It is important to state that God still releases miracles today, especially where the Kingdom is advancing into enemy-held territory. This speaks to a physical geography as well as an individual's life. Some of us think we should expect miracles as commonly as in the ministry of Jesus and his apostles. (e.g. John 14:12) Throughout the *Brit Chadasha* (New Testament) there are texts that authenticate the apostle's unique ministry (e.g. Hebrews 2:3-4; 2 Corinthians 12:12).

THE WORKING GEARS OF JEWISH EVANGELISM FOR DISCUSSION

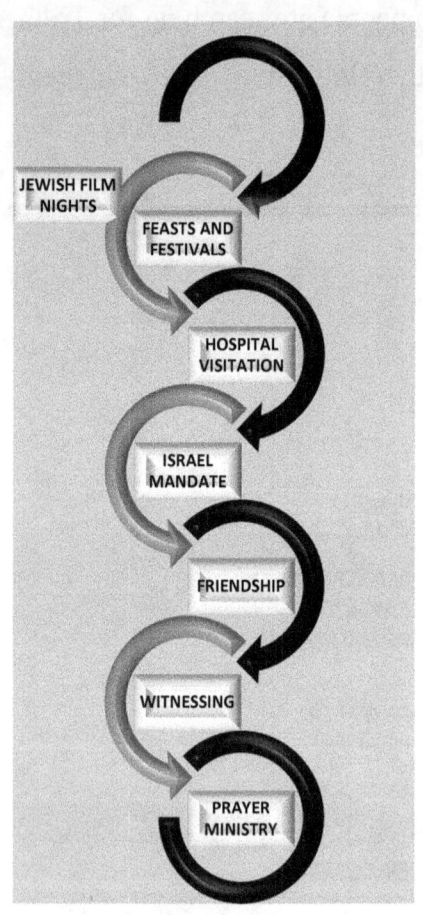

Jewish ministry provides many opportunities and venues to present the Gospel and show Messiah's love. One of the most exciting and effective is the **hosting of the Feasts, Holocaust Remembrance Night, Israel Mandate Events**, and **Jewish Film Nights**. These unique venues bring Jewish people into the local church where they can become comfortable in a gentile Christian environment. Also, these unique times can be opportunities to show deference to Jewish suffering and history, while demonstrating a love for the Jewish people.

- HOST A JEWISH FILM NIGHT FOR THE LOCAL JEWISH COMMUNITY.

- HOST A HOLOCAUST REMEMBRANCE NIGHT AND BRING IN A HOLOCAUST SURVIVOR.

- HOST AN ISRAEL MANDATE EVENING, "PRAYING FOR THE PEACE OF JERUSALEM."

- INVITE A JEWISH MINISTRY IN TO TEACH ON THE FEASTS AND PASSOVER.

- HOST JEWISH EVANGELISM SEMINARS TO TRAIN LAY PEOPLE IN WITNESSING TO JEWISH PEOPLE.

- LEARN TO WITNESS WITH CORRECT TERMINOLOGY.

- JEWISH PEOPLE LOVE TO RECEIVE PRAYER, VISIT A JEWISH FRIEND OR NEIGHBOR IN THE HOSPITAL

- ABOVE ALL, PRAY FOR JEWISH FRIENDS AND NEIGHBORS; PRAY FOR THE SALVATION OF THE JEWISH PEOPLE.

SECTION IV

NEW TESTAMENT

OLD TESTAMENT

WORDS FROM DR. MITCH GLASER

MEMORY BLOCK SET I:

MESSIAH'S BIRTH

PROVIDED HERE, IS A BRIEF INTRODUCTION TO THE ROMANS ROAD OF JEWISH EVANGELISM. ALSO, SOME OF THE KEY OLD TESTAMENT PROPHECIES. THE BOOK OF ROMANS IS UNSURPASSED WITH ITS TEACHINGS ON SUCH PRINCIPLES OF THE IRREVOCALBE CALL.

FIRST THINGS FIRST EVANGELISM: TO THE JEW FIRST, AND GODS ENDURING HEART FOR THE JEW TO COME TO FAITH SINCE THE FIRST ADVENT OF OUR MESSIAH.

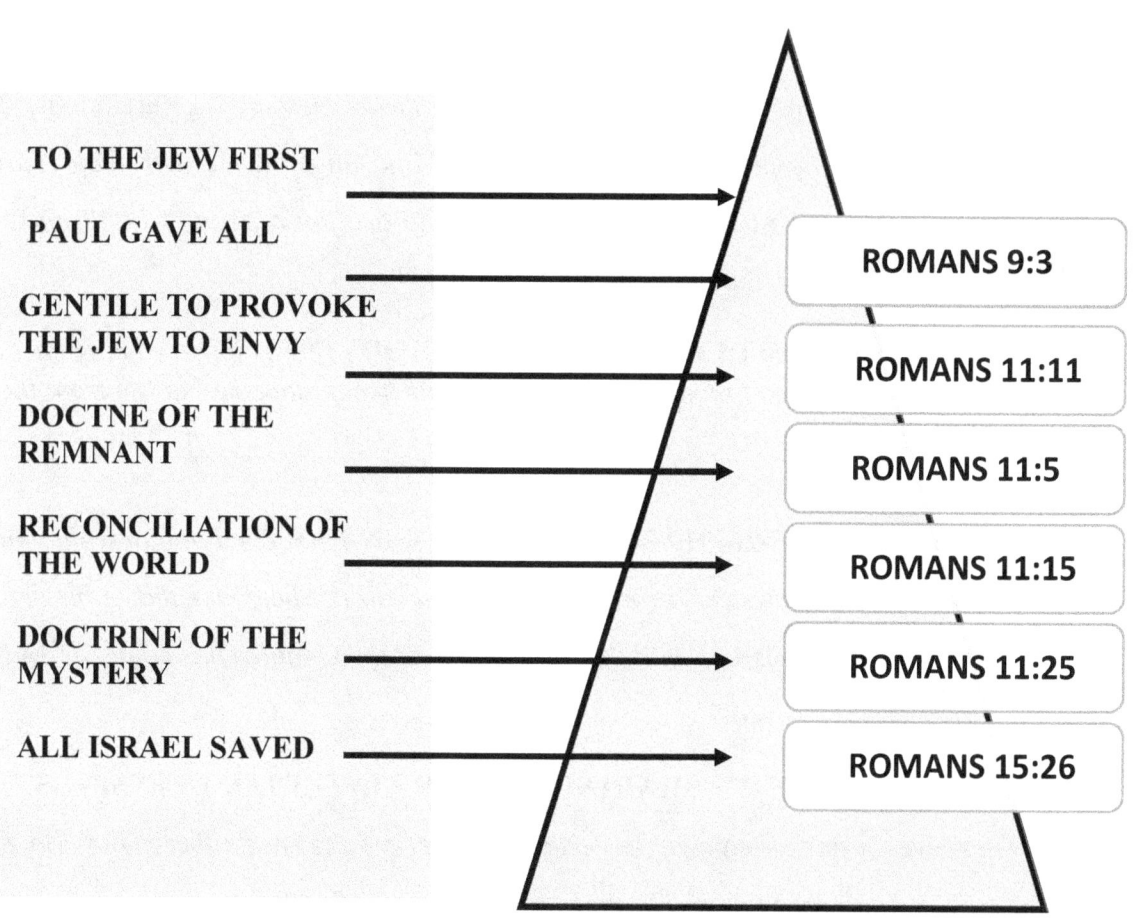

A. **ROMANS 1:16: TO THE JEW FIRST**: *"For I am not ashamed of the gospel of Christ, for it is the power of God to salvation for everyone who believes, for the Jew first and also for the Greek."*

B. **ROMANS 9:3: ADOPTION AS SONS:** *"For I could wish that I myself were cursed and cut off from Christ for the sake of my brothers, my own flesh, and blood, the people of Israel. Theirs is the adoption as sons; the divine glory and the covenants; theirs the giving of the Law, the temple worship, and the promises.*

C. **ROMANS 11:5: BY GRACE ALONE:** *"So too, at the present time there is a remnant chosen by grace. And if by grace, then it is no longer by works: If it were, grace would no longer be grace.*

D. **ROMANS 11:11: MAKE THE JEW ENVIOUS: "***Again I ask: Did they stumble so as to fall beyond recovery? Not at all! Rather, because of their transgression, salvation has come to the Gentiles to make Israel envious"*. Deuteronomy 32:21: *"They made me jealous by what is no god and angered me with their worthless idols. I will make them envious by those who are not a people; I will make them angry by a nation that has no understanding."*

E. **ROMANS 11:15: BLESSINGS TO THE BODY***: "For if there being cast away is the reconciling of the world, what will their acceptance be but life from the dead?"*

F. **ROMANS 11:25-26: HARDENING ONLY IN PART**: *"I do not want you to be ignorant of this mystery, brothers so that you will not be conceited: A hardening in part has come to Israel until the full number of the Gentiles has come in. And so all Israel shall be saved."*

G. **ROMANS 15:25-27: SHARING OF OUR MATERIAL BLESSINGS**: *"Now, however, I am on my way to Jerusalem to serve the saints there. For Macedonia and Achaia were pleased to make a contribution for the poor among the saints in Jerusalem. They were pleased to do it, and indeed they owe it to them. For if the

Gentiles have shared in their spiritual blessings, they are obligated to minister to hem with material blessings."

H. GENESIS 49:10: BORN BEFORE 70AD: *"The scepter will not depart from Judah, nor the ruler's staff from between his feet, until he to whom it belongs shall come and the obedience of the nations shall be His."*

NOTES:

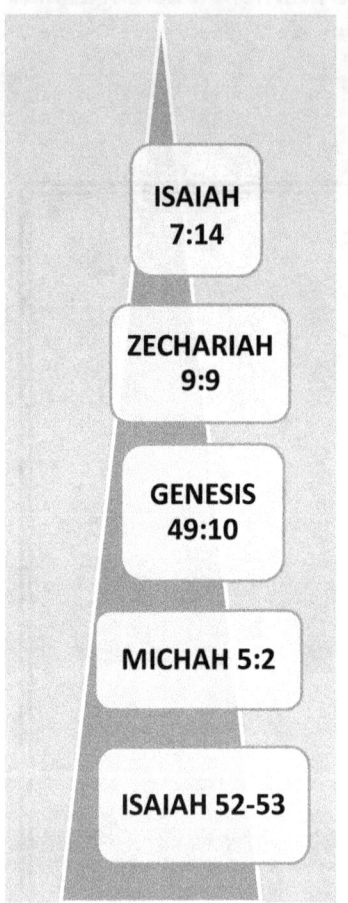

A. **ISAIAH 7:14: BORN OF A VIRGIN**: *"Therefore the Lord Himself will give you a sign: Behold, a virgin will be with child and bear a son, and she will call His name Immanuel."*

B. **ZECHARIAH 9:9: RIDING ON A DONKEY**: *"Rejoice greatly, Daughter Zion! Shout, Daughter Jerusalem! See, your king comes to you, righteous and victorious, lowly and riding on a donkey, on a colt, the foal of a donkey."*

C. **MICAH 5:2: BORN IN BETHLEHEM**: *"But you, Bethlehem Ephrathah, though you are little among the thousands of Judah, yet out of you shall come forth to Me, The One to be Ruler in Israel, whose goings forth are from of old."*

D. **GENESIS 49:10: BORN BEFORE 70AD:** *"The scepter will not depart from Judah, nor the ruler's staff from between his feet, until he to whom it belongs shall come and the obedience of the nations shall be His."*

CHOSEN PEOPLE MINISTRIES

DR. MITCH GLASER

THE JEWISH people cannot comprehend how a person can be a Jew and a Christian at the same time. They presume that if they accept Jesus they can no longer be Jewish.

THE JEWISH people are not especially religious. Most modern Jews value the traditional and cultural elements of their heritage more than the religious. In fact, synagogue attendance in the United States is below 15%!

THE JEWISH people are taught to reject certain essential teachings of the Bible such as the Trinity, the deity of the Messiah, and the Second Coming of Jesus.

THE JEWISH people are not especially familiar with the Old Testament. Most would question whether the Bible was even inspired by God. Orthodox Jews do accept the Scriptures, but most modern and secular Jewish people do not accept the divine authority of their own Old Testament.

THE JEWISH people are surprised to hear that Jesus was Jewish and the New Testament was written by Jews. They view the New Testament as a "non-Jewish book that has spawned another world religion. Some even think Jesus was a nice Jewish boy who converted to Christianity!

THE JEWISH people intuitively know that if they were to consider Jesus, their families and friends would not understand them, and some might even disown them. We see an example of this in John 9, where the Jewish leaders threatened the parents of the blind man with excommunication if they acknowledged that Jesus had healed their son.

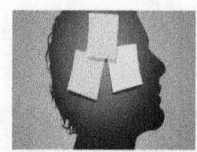

"I know of no other single practice in the Christian life more rewarding, practically speaking, than memorizing Scripture. No other single exercise pays greater spiritual dividends! Your prayer life will be strengthened. Your witnessing will be sharper and much more effective. Your attitudes and outlook will begin to change. Your mind will become alert and observant. Your confidence and assurance will be enhanced. Your faith will be solidified."

- **Chuck Swindoll**

PLACE OF BIRTH: Micah 5:2, *"But you, Bethlehem Ephrata, though you are little among the thousands of Judah, yet out of you shall come forth to Me the One to be Ruler in Israel, whose goings forth are from of old,"*

MANNER OF BIRTH: Isaiah 7:14, *"Therefore the Lord Himself will give you a sign: Behold, the virgin shall conceive and bear a Son, and shall call His name Immanuel."*

TIME OF BIRTH: Genesis 49:10; 5:2, *"The scepter will not depart from Judah, nor the ruler's staff from between his feet, until he to whom it belongs shall come and the obedience of the nations shall be his."*

PROPHETIC/EVANGELISM: In 1 Corinthians 14:1-3, Paul tells us to *"pursue love, yet earnestly desire spiritual gifts, but especially that you may prophesy."* Translated literally, it means that we should "lust" after prophecy. But why is prophecy so important that we should pursue it?

-

SECTION V

HISTORICAL ACTS JEWISH ANTI-SEMITISM

WHY JEWISH PEOPLE DO NOT BELIEVE IN JESUS

SIX "C" WORDS THAT BECAME A SWORD AGAINST THE JEW

VOICES OF JEWISH HATE AND CHRISTIAN RULINGS

AMERICAN ANTI-SEMITISM

TERMS FOR EFFECTIVE OUTREACH

HISTORICAL ANTISEMTISM

I

 Understanding how some of the most important words in Christianity became a source of persecution and pain to Jewish people enables those interested in sharing their faith with Jewish people, to understand Jewish objection to the Christian message. Here we highlight 6 "C" words that are provocative but for the wrong reason. Numerous church leaders early on carried a message of Jewish hate that fostered an anti-Semitic environment for centuries. Finally, we end this section with an introduction of anti-Semitism that was present in the colonial days of America, and how it impacted notable individuals.

When sharing the Gospel with Jewish people, it may seem odd and perhaps even heretical to refrain from using such terms as, ***Cross, Christ, Church, Christian, Crusade, and also, Conversion***. One might compare it to giving someone a hammer and then telling them to go build a house, but they cannot have the nails. How do we do it? How do the Jewish people discover their Yeshua without those "Nails"?

Immediately, one discovers that Jewish evangelism is perhaps one of the most miss-understood, time-consuming, and challenging harvest fields. The Church's history as understood by Jewish People is filled with prejudice, bigotry, and historical suffering. The damage done in the name of Christ and Christianity has been almost immeasurable. From Hitler's plan to destroy the Jewish people as a Christian mission, to crosses displayed over his ovens, Luther's venomous spouts of anti-Semitism, along with Christian leaders and their anti-Semitic sermons, ignited a broad range of anti-Semitic rulings. Most of these were done by the Catholic Church down through history.

For this reason, we provide six replacement terms at the end of this section for an individual to employ when speaking with Jewish people about *Yeshua*, (Jesus) our Messiah. An additional challenge is faced in Jewish Ministry to rectify a two-part historical dilemma:

- **CHRISTIANITY IS NOT SEEN AS A RELIGION OF LOVE:** Numerous influential individuals spread prejudice the early church towards Jews through anti-Jewish thinking and theologies which we explore in this section. Walls of separation were erected between the Jew and the New Covenant Church, and their teachings steered generations away from any concept of God's intended relationship between the Jew and the Gentile. These early mindsets and prejudices became a pretext for Jewish and Christian relations for centuries. Hence, wrought by a history greatly framed by anti-Semitism in early Christian history, much effort should be given to education, preparation, and prayer.

- **JEWS THINK THEY CANNOT BE JEWISH IF THEY BELIEVE IN YESHUA.** One should always seek to place *Yeshua* back into His original Jewish framework. This is done to demonstrate that historically, culturally, and Biblically, believing in the Messiah is the most Jewish decision that a Jewish person can make. Therefore, taking the time to prepare as a missionary spends before reaching his or her field is important to the success of Jewish ministry. This empowers the believer to be a sensitive and loving witness and one that is empowered to fulfill the mandate to the Jew as stated in Romans 11:11, *"for the purpose of Gentile salvation is to provoke to the Jewish to envy."*

[CHRISTIAN HISTORY]

Sadly, episodes of conflict and contention existed in the early Christian and the Jewish world, which shaped an overwhelming schism between Jewish and Christian relations. A systematic inertia was flowing towards anti-Semitism early on. This did not occur through one specific event or individual, but through repetitive episodes over time. Hence, numerous church leaders poisoned these words through a deeply flawed interpretive reasoning. It profaned God's heart for Israel and the Jewish people. Of course, at its root was satan who is the author of all Jewish hate!

FLAWED REASONING CREATES ANTI-JEWISH THEOLOGIES. Supersessionism or the dark interpretative reasoning and *Replacement theology* are philosophies suggested that the Gentile Church replaced physical Israel, and a new spiritual Israel was created, which became the new Gentile Christian Church. Essentially, the Gentile Christian replaced the Jew. Then the blessings spoken of in the Bible regarding the Jew were consigned over to the Gentile but cursing and wrath remained squarely upon the shoulders of the Jewish people. As a result, Israel and the Jewish people lost their covenantal inheritance. Their distinction and calling were revoked, and the Jew would no longer be a people and nation carried over from God's covenant with Abraham. This reasoning further caused obvious Jewish prejudice in Christianity. Individuals emerged that caused a deep divide between the Jew and the Gentile, and the New Covenant Church.

MORE VOICES OF JEWISH HATE

We limit our remarks not to Luther. Down through the age many leaders set the stage for others to stumble as well. Certainly, Hitler was unsurpassed. But some of the notorious acts that he undertook were inspirited by Christian history itself. For instance, the labeling of the Jew with a yellow star as is one example. Below we offer a short list of other voices that spoke out against the Jewish people.

> **John Chrysostom** (334–407 AD) was a bishop of the Church of Antioch and was considered the greatest preacher of his day and spoke violently against the Jews. He said, "There could never be forgiveness for the Jews, and that God had always hated them." He taught that it was the Christian duty to hate

the Jews, that the Jews were assassins of Christ, that their synagogues were worse than brothels, and likened them to demons devoted to idolatrous cults.

Justin Martyr (100–165 AD) claimed that God's covenant with the Jews was no longer valid and that Gentiles had replaced the Jewish people in God's redemptive plan, (Replacement Theology).

Ignatius (35-108 AD) was the bishop of the church in Antioch in the second century; he wrote that anyone who celebrated Passover with the Jews or received emblems of the Jewish feast was a partaker with those who killed the Lord and His apostles.

Clement of Alexandria (150–AD 215 AD) emphasized Greek philosophy rather than the *Tanakh* as the primary means that God gave to the Gentiles to lead the Jewish people to Jesus as the ultimate Word of God.

Tertullian (160–AD 220 AD) was one of the most important Christian writers of the second century; his works were highly significant in developing the basic doctrines of today's church. In one of his writings, titled *Against the Jews,* he blamed the entire Jewish race for the death of Jesus.

Eusebius (263–AD 339 AD) taught that the promises and blessings of the *Tanakh* (Old Testament) were the Christians and that the curses were for the Jews. He declared that the church was the "true Israel of God" that had replaced literal Israel in God's covenants.

Jerome (345–AD 420 AD) was a great Bible scholar whose Latin translation of the Scriptures became the official Bible of the church. Jerome claimed that the Jews were incapable of understanding the Scriptures and that they should be severely persecuted until they confessed to the "true faith."

Throughout Catholic Church history, numerous anti-Semitic actions, and rulings as those noted were undertaken which show the Jewish people: Christianity was again a religion of anti-Jewish hate. Review the following list of further rulings:

1. **AD 589**: Jews were forbidden from holding public office.

2. **AD 612–621**: King Sisebut forced either baptism or exile.

3. **AD 570–636**: Saint Isadore forbade forced baptisms, but if children were baptized to save their lives, they had to be taken from their parents and reared Catholic. In some situations, Jewish people were given a choice of baptism or death.

4. **AD 692**: Christians were not permitted to patronize Jewish doctors.

5. **AD 1078**: Jews were required to pay taxes for the support of the Roman Church to the same extent as Christians.

6. **AD 1060**: The First Crusade against the Jews that killed thousands who refused baptism.

7. **AD 1146**: Second Crusade, the same took place.

8. **AD 1267**: Christians were not allowed to attend Jewish ceremonies.

9. **AD 1357**: During the Black Death, Jews were accused of poisoning the wells, thus causing the plague. Some of this may have come from the fact that many Jewish people were observing the health laws of *Tanakh* and, were thus not getting sick (Toledo, 681).

1. In what way can the knowledge of the historical persecutions of the Jewish people make your witness to the Jewish people more effective?

2. Why is it important to employ such replacement terms as given in this section?

3. Give six examples of modern-day Anti-Semitism in the Church.

4. Give three biblical examples of anti-Semitism increasing in the last days, and what opportunity is presented to the end time church to take actions against it.

MINISTER TO THE POOR AND NEEDY: Isaiah 61:1-2; Luke 4:16-*21 "The Spirit of the Lord GOD is upon me, Because the LORD has anointed me to bring good news to the afflicted; He has sent me to bind up the brokenhearted, to proclaim liberty to captives, and freedom to prisoners; To proclaim the favorable year of the Lord, and the day of vengeance of our God. To comfort all those who mourn."*

REJCTED BY HIS OWN: Isaiah 53:3 **"***He was despised and rejected by mankind, a man of suffering, and familiar with pain. Like one from whom people hide their faces he was despised, and we held him in low esteem."*

WORKER OF MIRACLES: Isaiah 35:5-6; Matthew 11:1-6 *"Then the eyes of the blind shall be opened, and the ears of the deaf shall be unstopped. Then the lame shall leap like a deer, and the tongue of the dumb sing. For waters shall burst forth in the wilderness, and streams in the desert."*

ACKNOWLEDGED BY MANY: Zechariah 9:9; Matthew 21:4-*9 "Rejoice greatly, Daughter of Zion! Shout, Daughter Jerusalem! See, your king comes to you, righteous and victorious, lowly and riding on a donkey, on a colt, the foal of a donkey."*

HERALD BY A FORERUNNER: Isaiah 40:10; Malachi 3:1: *"See, the Sovereign LORD comes with power, and he rules with a mighty arm. See, his reward is with him, and his recompense accompanies him."*

HISTORICAL ANTISEMITISM
II

"Short of the Auschwitz oven and extermination, the whole Nazi Holocaust is pre-outlined here." Is it any wonder that Hitler and Julius Striecher quoted Martin Luther as justification for the destruction of 6 million Jews?

SIX "C" WORDS THAT BECAME A SWORD OF OFFENSE

Church / Christian / Cross / Conversion / Crusade / Christ

"If we hear all this suffering and if there are still Jews left, when it is over, then Jews, instead of being doomed, will be held up as an example."

— Anne Frank

REPLACEMENT TERMS

CHRIST
- Yeshua
- Messiah

CHURCH
- Congregation
- Assembly
- Meeting

CHRISTIAN
- Believer
- Follower

CROSS	CONVERSION	CRUSADES
Forgiveness Redemption	• COMPLETION • FUFILLMENT	Never use the term, Crusades

CHURCH: Congregation, or Assembly, Gathering, Service.

CHRISTIAN: Believer; a follower of Messiah, or, Jesus the Jewish Messiah.

CROSS: A difficult topic to contend with at first, because it often requires explanation, and most importantly, a relationship to bring clarity and understanding to a Jewish person. But terms to use are *redemption* and *atonement*.

CRUSADES: Never use this term! This represents some of the most notorious and insufferable of acts against the Jewish people.

CONVERSION: A better term is completion or fulfillment. The term conversion describes the supernatural work that Jesus performs in both Jew and Gentile. Still, Jews are not converted to being Gentile Christians, any more than Gentile believers become Jewish. Jewish belief in Messiah is a work of "fulfillment," or "completion, and not conversion."

CHRIST: Messiah, *Yeshua. Yeshua* is Jesus' Hebrew name, and as noted in the edition of Power Books, we are always working to restore a Jewish context to New Covenant terms, which history has infused with prejudice and anti-Jewish hate. (This ***topic requires explanation and discussion).***

HISTORICAL ANTI-SEMITISM
III

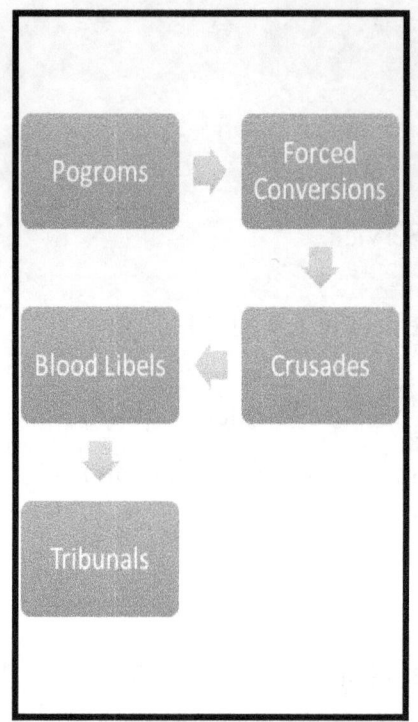

This section begins to build a foundation for understanding.

The most common anti-Semitic acts in history took the form of the following: *Forced Conversions, Pogroms, Blood Libels, Crusades, and Tribunals*. These were historical, and infamous assaults on the Jew and, often, done in the name of a Christian mission. But of course, it was blatant anti-Jewish hate.

Many generations followed that Generations possessed little understanding of God's intended relationship between the Jew and the Gentile and the church and Israel. The historical and theological pretexts were formed creating a trajectory that was constantly moving away from any Jewish foundation. When wanting to proclaim the Gospel to the Jew, this historical awareness in Judaism is often confronted. And if the Gospel message of Messiah is to impact larger populations of Jewish people, the understanding of these histories will be paramount, coupled with tangible demonstrations of love.

[ALWAYS BEING EXILED]

We begin with a simple introduction to the Jewish people and their history. Throughout history, the Jews have been hated and exiled from most places, and few people other than Jews have experienced this historical reality. Until 1948, Jews have been scattered. Their wanderings throughout the nations have defined them for thousands of years, and it explains why Jews can be found in every nation on earth. Few nations, however, are free from the particular bloodguilt of being unwelcoming to Jewish people.

European nations were infamous for this that included England, France, Germany, Portugal, Spain, Lithuania, and Hungary. These nations displaced untold thousands of Jews. In 1492, 90,000

Jews from Turkey were forced to leave their homes. During that same period, thousands were forcibly baptized in Spain, and thousands more that refused were exiled.

When you combine all of the various episodes of Jewish prejudice, hundreds of thousands of Jews were displaced, thousands more died seeking a new home, and thousands more underwent forced conversions and baptisms.[i] One can only imagine what Spanish Jewry of the era thought of the Jewish Psalm 60: *"O God, thou hast cast us off, thou hast scattered us, thou hast been displeased; O turn thyself to us again"* (KJV).

[BRANDED AS DIFFERENT]

Sadly, while the term "exile" defined much of Jewish history, Jews have long been branded by society as "different," thereby casting shame upon them. Portrayed as modern-day money mongers, or from fables depicting Jews as having horns, Jews were always viewed as different from Gentiles. When Jews were forced to wear special labels to tell them apart from Gentiles, however, it was a practice that was both notorious, and demeaning. It also began to lay the groundwork for a pattern in history.

THE CATHOLIC CHURCH FIRST PRACTICED IT, AND ADOLPH HITLER COPIED IT:

In 1215, the Catholic Church issued a decree at the 4th Lateran Council that all Jews were required to wear a yellow badge upon their breast to distinguish them from Gentile Christians. In 1317, the Catholic Church at the Ravenna Council declared the following: "That they (Jews) ought not to be tolerated to the detriment or severe injury of the faithful because it frequently happens that they return to Christian's contumely for favors, contempt for familiarity.

> The provincial of Ravenna some time since thinking that many scandals have arisen from them commingling with Christians, decreed that they should wear a wheel of yellow cloth on their outer garment. Their women were forced to wear a wheel on their heads so that they may be distinguished from Christians."[ii]

One can immediately notice the complexity and brevity of Jewish persecutions that began to poison the well of Christianity. Mel Gibson in 2004 illustrated in his movie the Passion of the Christ one effect. Although it was deeply passionate from a Gentile Christian perspective, it was a troubling reminder to Jewish people of how they were treated by Christianity down through history and evoked painful memories and images from the Shoah (the Holocaust). The Gentile Christian approaches such stories vastly different than a Jewish person. The Gospels tell the story of the life and ministry of Jesus, the Messiah, the Savior who suffered and died to rise to new life. It is a story of sacrifice and love.

By the same token, most Gentile believers are unaware of how this story resonates with many Jewish people. The average Christian is not well acquainted with Jewish history and, equally, the history of Christian anti-Judaism in particular. Those things that most concern the Jewish community are simply not on the radar screen for Christians. Consider the following Church leaders in history that influenced not only their generation but also hundreds that followed.

[MESSENGERS OF JEWISH HATE]

One of the most villainous was Martin Luther (AD 1483-1546). But wait a minute Rabbi, didn't he begin the Reformation, and bring the Christian Church out of a period of deep darkness? Yes!

✡ **IN 1523, MARTIN LUTHER WROTE AN ARTICLE ENTITLED,** *"THAT CHRIST WAS BORN A JEW."* In 1523, Martin Luther's article harshly criticized the Catholic Church for presenting a pagan brand of Christianity to the Jews. He expressed empathy for the Jews and said, "If I had been a Jew and had seen such fools and blockheads teach the Christian faith, I should rather have turned into a pig than become a Christian?

Though Luther was celebrated for birthing the Protestant Reformation, he became embittered towards the Jewish people when they constantly resisted his efforts to convert them to Christianity. He began to pour out

venomous sermons against them that were a pure display of anti-Jewish hate; sermons that are renowned in Judaism. Even the Encyclopedia Judaica writes of Luther, "Short of the Auschwitz oven and extermination; the whole Nazi Holocaust is pre-outlined here. Is it any wonder then, that Hitler and Julius Streicher quoted Martin Luther as justification for their destruction of 6 million Jews?"

[MARTIN LUTHER'S SERMONS]

WHAT SHALL WE CHRISTIANS DO WITH THIS DAMNED REJECTED RACE OF JEWS? Since they live among us and we know about their lying, blasphemy, and cursing, we cannot tolerate them if we do not wish to share in their lies, curses, and blasphemy. In this way, we cannot quench the fire of divine rage (as the prophets say) nor convert the Jews." He went on to say, "Prayerfully and reverentially we must practice a merciful severity. Perhaps we may save a few from the fire and the flames. We must not seek vengeance. They are surely being punished a thousand times more than we might wish them. Let me give you my honest advice."

- ✡ Their synagogues or churches should be set on fire, and whatever does not burn up should be covered or spread over with dirt so that no one may ever be able to see a cinder or stone of it. This ought to be done for the honor of God and Christianity so that God may see that we are Christians and that we have not wittingly tolerated or approved, of such public lying, cursing, and blaspheming of His Son and His Christians.

- ✡ Their houses should likewise be broken down and destroyed. For they perpetrate the same things there that they do in their synagogues. For this reason, they ought to be put under one roof or in a stable, like gypsies, so that they may realize that they are not masters in our land, as they boast, but miserable captives, as they complain of us incessantly before God with their bitter wailing.

- ✡ They should be deprived of their prayer books and Talmud's in which such idolatry, lies, cursing, and blasphemy are taught.

✡ Their rabbis must be forbidden under threat of death to teach anymore.

✡ Passports and traveling privileges should be absolutely forbidden to Jews. For they have no business in the rural districts since they are not nobles, nor officials, nor merchants, nor the like. Let them stay at home.

✡ They ought to be stopped from usury. All their cash and valuables of silver and gold ought to be taken from them and put aside for safekeeping. For this reason, everything that they possess they stole and robbed from us through their usury, for they have no other means of support. This money should be used in the case (and in no other) where a Jew has honestly become a Christian, so that he may get for the time being one or two or three hundred florins, as the person may require. This in order, that he may start a business to support his poor wife and children and the old and feeble. Such evilly acquired money is cursed, unless, with God's blessing, it is put to some good and necessary use.

POGROMS: *Pogrom* is a Russian word that means riot, hundreds of *Pogroms* in large such anti-Jewish riots took place especially under the Czarist regime of Russia and Poland. Too Russian authorities, Jews represented a "Jewish problem." This was regularly met with forced conversions, amounting to one-third of the Jewish population, and emigration of another third. This took place in an intensified manner from 1881-1921.

BLOOD LIBEL: *Blood libel* is a lie or fable that accuses Jews of taking a Christian child's blood for ritual purposes; specifically, taking the blood to make matzo for Passover. This of course is ridiculous since the Jewish people observe Torah, and from the kosher laws in Leviticus 11, it is forbidden to ingest the blood of an animal, let alone a human being.

TRIBUNALS: The most feared and hated word is Inquisition, which literally means "inquiry." Specifically, Jews were forced to convert to Christianity during the Spanish Inquisition over the course of the fifteenth and sixteenth centuries. Hundreds of thousands of Jews were killed in a frenzy of hateful anti-Jewish violence. Again, all this was done in the name of Christ.

CRUSADES: One of the darkest times for the Jewish people took place during the Crusades. These were undertaken as military expeditions under the blessing of the church to recover the Holy Land from the Muslims and Jews. During these episodes, Jews were herded into synagogues, and while the Crusaders sang, *"Christ We Adore Thee,"* they would set fire to the synagogue, burning the Jews alive. The Battle cry of the Crusaders was as follows; "Before attempting to avenge ourselves upon the Muslim unbelievers, let us first avenge ourselves upon the *killers of Christ in our midst."*

FORCED CONVERSIONS: Taking Jewish children at the complete disregard of their parents in order to convert them is reprehensible. But episodes as those mentioned took place throughout Europe, Persia, and Morocco from 460 AD to as late as 1858. The Canonist decree during the nineteenth century by Russian authorities was the most notorious. Children were seized and forced to serve in the czar's army. Then they were shipped off to distant locations for as much as twenty-five years. The purpose was to force Jewish children to lose all contact with their people in order assimilate and convert them to the local religion.

- Most persecutions came from Christian anti-Semitism.
- Many acts of hatred and brutality came in the name of Jesus or under the banner of the Cross.

- During these episodes, Jews were herded into synagogues, and while the Crusaders sang, "Christ We Adore The".

- The majority of Christian Anti-Semitic acts came by the Catholic church; hence many Jewish people see Christians in the light of Catholicism.

PERSONAL EXPERIENCE WITH JEWISH PREJUDICE

AMERICAN ACTS OF ANTI-SEMITISM

"The question shouldn't be 'Why are you, a Christian, here in a death camp, condemned for trying to save Jews?' The real question is "Why aren't all the Christians here?"

― Joel C. Rosenberg, The Auschwitz Escape

ADOLPH HITLER: *Hence today I believe that I am acting in accordance with the will of the Almighty Creator: 'by defending myself against the Jew, I am fighting for the work of the Lord.' -Adolf Hitler (Mein Kampf.)*

Although one has called the Holocaust, "The emptying out of a great moral space from the world", Hitler had a solution to solve what he saw as the Jewish problem, called the "final solution." His plan to exterminate all of European Jewry almost succeeded. Six million Jewish lives were lost. Some of those were my paternal grandparents, uncles, aunts, and cousins and, for untold other Jewish families, the same.

Hitler's propaganda machine claimed that the vileness of Jews was part of their blood; that they were inferior, physically, mentally and, culturally. Jews, he said, "polluted modern life with filth and disease. They poisoned others with germs, but somehow managed to preserve themselves." German society was infected by Jewish hate to such degrees that a board game was created for Germans called Jews Get Out. This game was sold throughout Germany in 1939 and 1940. In 1938, a children's anti-Semitic book was published called *The Poisonous Mushroom* through which German children could be inculcated with anti-Jewish hate. Throughout Germany, there were public signs warning women and girls to watch out for the rapist, the Jew! Other public signs were posted as "Beware of Jews and pickpockets." Four hundred laws and decrees were created by Hitler, which defined what a "non-Aryan" is: A non-Aryan was anyone descended from non-Aryan, especially Jewish, parents or grandparents, even if only one parent or grandparent was a non-Aryan. Following this policy, every government worker in Germany had to prove his or her lineage.

[AMERICAN ANTI-SEMITISM]

We now turn our attention briefly to America. As she became a haven for many people groups during pre-colonial times, Jews were also seeking a place of religious freedom. It seems she was not quite ready for them. During this early period of American history, early settlers were rugged and hardworking, and mostly farmers and ranchers. The early Jewish settlers were known to be more a people of the city. Principally, business people and artisans. They worked as hard as everyone else, but they just channeled their efforts differently. Still, throughout this early period, Jews were viewed as reaping the fruits of others' hard labor.

More central, though, America was seen as a new Christian nation, and Jews were still viewed as Christ killers, a label carried over from England. During this period in the early American frontier, Jewish prejudices continued throughout the colonies. Conversion to Christianity however always seemed to be the accepted practice on rectifying the Jewish problem. Consider the following people and groups in early America and their attitudes.

[PURITANS]

In Boston where the Puritans settled, they thought that they were the real Jews and genuine heirs of the promises that God gave to the Jews. Three generations after the beginning of the northern colonies, Samuel Willard outlined Puritan sentiments in a sermon that he preached in 1700: "The Jews were a scorn and reproach to the world: the happy day of the conversion could improve their condition." [2] The Puritans saw the "end of days" upon them, and they believed the second coming could not happen unless most Jews were converted.

---

[2] Arthur Hertzberg: The Jews in America; four centuries of an uneasy encounter; Simon * Shuster 1989.

[HANNAH ADAMS]

A descendant of Henry Adams, and a distant cousin of John Adams, Hannah published a work on the history of the Jews in 1812. In her view of history, the suffering of the Jews is due to their rejection of Christ. Adams accuses the Jews of continuing to regard themselves as "the chosen people," and "superior" to all others."[3] More important, what Hannah Adams believed was the general view in America, and that American freedom for the Jew was an opportunity for them to be converted to an enlightened Christianity.

[THOMAS JEFFERSON]

One of the founding fathers of America revealed ambivalence toward the Jews when he said, "They should labor to achieve equality in science that is in secular learning so that they will become objects of respect and favor."[iii] Later, Thomas Jefferson was more positive toward them, and their religious rights, especially after the Bill of Rights and the Constitution. Thomas Jefferson was, in fact, the one who incorporated the principle of separation of church and state into the Constitution. He said, "Building a wall of separation between church and state, and that religion is a matter solely between a man and God."[iv]

[HENRY FORD]

Henry Ford, one of the great American industrialists and automaker was a major trumpet of anti-Semitism in his day. *The Protocols of the Elders of Zion* published a generation earlier, and most likely originated from the secret police of the Russian czar, was aimed at justifying anti-Semitic policies, and was published in the United States in 1919. Henry Ford financed the production of hundreds of thousands of copies. The publication asserted that the Jews were part of a conspiracy to dominate the world. On this basis, Ford's paper became the chief voice of anti-Semitism in America during the 1920s.

---

[3] Seth S. Wenger, *The Jewish Americans: Three Centuries of Jewish Voices in America.* Doubleday Publishers 2007

[YALE AND HARVARD]

Education for Jewish people was always paramount and entering prominent institutions of higher learning before the early 1920s went largely unhindered. A problem began, however, when a growing number of universities began to feel uneasy with an increasing Jewish presence and, increasingly, Jews began to out-perform many of their gentile classmates.

Quotas soon began to be instituted in places like Harvard, Princeton, and Yale. Harvard President A. Lawrence Lowell said in 1922, "If every college in the country would take a limited proportion of Jews we should go a long way toward eliminating race feeling amongst our students." Lowell was later forced to retract his statement, but Jewish enrollment was mysteriously curtailed sharply after the incident.

At Yale, a decision was made that students should be admitted on the basis of character rather than just scholarship. Dean Frederick Jones at Yale University found that a Jew won almost every single scholarship of any value. He stated, "In terms of scholarship and intelligence Jewish students lead the class, but their personal characteristics make them markedly inferior." Of course, this so-called inferiority was only remedied by conversion to Christianity. [v]

When it came to medical schools' Jewish enrollment was discouraged. Jewish quotas forced thousands to go abroad for medical training. Gentiles controlled virtually all hospitals as well as the entire medical profession during the turn of the century. It was virtually impossible to find a Jewish doctor on a hospital staff or a Jewish professor in an American medical school. Consequently, the field was virtually closed to Jewish students seeking medical degrees.

[CONCLUSION]

Perhaps you have seen for the first time the atrocities, as well as anti-Jewish actions that have been taken against the Jewish people throughout the centuries. Now you realize the challenges facing Jewish outreach. We should feel disgust and anger towards those who would do such horrible things. For this reason, it is important for Christians to understand the world's past dealings with the Jewish people so that they will develop sensitivity towards Israel and the Jewish people.

Praise God that our mission to reach the "lost Sheep of the house of Israel" today, has become empowered by a love for the Jewish people on the part of Christian Church. As more and more come to understand the mishaps of Christian Church history, deep healing between Jews and Gentile Christians will be realized. Both are coming to a greater understanding of each other as they discover that their histories and destinies are intertwined. In reaching the Jewish people then, particularly in the context of so much openness today, it is incumbent upon us to reach out with actions, terminologies, temperaments, and proper training that embody the love of our Messiah.

Toward this end, we have listed alternative terms to the 6 "C" words at the conclusion of this topic. Individuals can easily integrate them into their vocabulary. Followed by much prayer and preparation, we can begin to engage Jewish people with confidence, an anointing with sensitivity. Truly, *"now is the time to show favor to her, the appointed time has come."* Psalms 102:13.

1. Given the broad range of Anti-Semitic acts in the name of Christianity, what can we do to foster trust and openness as we present the Gospel message of Messiah?

2. What steps can a church take to build bridges to the local Jewish community and how can one best present the truth of Messiah? What is the difference between "Conversion," and "Completion?"

SECTION VI

- SEVEN QUESTIONS ABOUT JUDAISM

- RABBI MYRON SLOBIN

- JEWISH OBJECTIONS TO CHRISTIAN MESSIANIC CLAIMS

- JEWISH HISTORY

- WHY JEWISH PEOPLE DO NOT BELIEVE IN JESUS

 Jew's love to ask questions! Listed here are 7 questions pertaining to Judaism that represent common questions that non-Jewish people ask. Also presented, are traditional objections to Christian belief by Jewish people, with a brief word on Jewish history and its influence upon Jewish evangelism.

> *"One only loves the Holy One blessed be He through the knowledge of Him. This love is commensurate to the knowledge. If the knowledge is little, the love will be little; and if the knowledge is great, the love will be great. Thus, it is imperative for a person to dedicate himself to understand and contemplate the wisdom and knowledge that inform him of his Creator."*
>
> **- Mishneh Torah, Hilchot Teshuvah 10:6**

It is highly likely you have encountered Jewish people and know a Jewish person. Your best friend may even be Jewish. Still, some things about their Judaism may seem curious. Your first thought is that they are the people of the Old Testament, chosen by God, so they must have a profound knowledge of the Scriptures. Well, you have probably discovered also that the answer to this is usually no.

Although God did choose them, their understanding of the Old Testament is, in most cases, seriously deficient. Furthermore, since Christians believe Jesus is the Messiah, and Jews do not, some think this is the only difference between Christianity and Judaism. However, there is much to consider when it comes to what Jewish people believe and do not believe; how Jewish people see Christians trying to convert them; why Jewish people are reluctant to trust Christians. The following provides some insight before we present the seven questions of Judaism. Take a few moments to meditate upon the following remarks from Rabbi Myron Slobin, a co-worker, and dear friend. Rabbi Myron notes from his own experience in Messianic Ministry and working with Jews for Jesus the following considerations.

 In the following seven questions of Judaism, one must understand that an entire theology is associated with believing in Jesus that Jews see as diametrically opposed to what their Bible states.

- Judaism is complex, comprised of great disparities from one sect to the other, something so foundational as Torah is not universally accepted or interpreted the same way from one to the other. Rather, different streams of thought intricately intertwine with traditional views, and they can depart from the main cloth to form their own fiber, yet, they can remain Jewish.

- Judaism is very much a religion and culture in motion from generation to generation. It is defined by a broad spectrum of belief, from complete secularism and humanism, to no faith in the One True God and Torah, to very deep religious rituals and beliefs. Some know more about the Bible than others. Some are absent from any knowledge of the Scriptures. In Orthodox Judaism, the ideal to garner wisdom comes from the Talmud and Mishnah.

- Judaism transformed itself after the Second Temple was destroyed in or around 70 AD, thereby creating more disparities that have endured to this day. Tackling this topic can be challenging given the limited work in this booklet. In this edition of Power Books, we highlight the seven fundamental questions about Judaism and provide in the Appendices, material for further reading and study.

SEVEN QUESTIONS ABOUT JUDAISM

1. **DO JEWISH PEOPLE BELIEVE IN REPENTANCE?** The Jewish principle of repentance or in Hebrew, *Teshuvah* (to return,) is different from Christianity. In Judaism, no savior is needed as an intermediary to mitigate one's personal sin and separation from God. Yet, the Jewish laws of repentance and substitution are so prominent in the book of Leviticus that modern Judaism sees no necessity for a blood sacrifice to achieve repentance, whether this is through an individual, or the blood of an animal, the concept of one's salvation from sin through *Yeshua's* sacrifice is a foreign concept.

   - *Jews believe in an individual and collective involvement with God through tradition, rituals, prayers, and ethical actions. Repentance does take place, but once per year on Yom Kippur. On that day, they believe a special window is open to them whereby God, through their involvement in Yom Kippur, prayers, and fasting, receive the forgiveness that lasts for the next year.*

2. **DO JEWISH PEOPLE BELIEVE IN THE TRINITY?** Another significant distinction between Christianity and Judaism is the Godhead or Trinity. In Judaism, there is no belief in a Triune God. The thought of one person, although divine, coming in human form, is considered heretical and a blasphemous principle.

   > Two thousand years ago, the Pharisees viewed and treated *Yeshua* with disdain and revulsion over this very issue when He claimed to have come from the Father. Judaism, on the other hand, emphasizes the Oneness of God without three distinct operations. This belief has been rehearsed for thousands of years in the Shema, which is the most ancient declaration of Judaism. It affirms Judaism's faith in one God; *"Hear O Israel the Lord your God, the Lord is One,"* (Deuteronomy 6:4-9).

3. **DO JEWISH PEOPLE BELIEVE IN HEAVEN AND HELL?** Generally speaking, Judaism does not teach a particular concept of hell. It is assumed that evildoers will be punished. But the manner and place of chastisement are left to the justice of God. Although the Old Testament clearly teaches a place of eternal suffering and torment, (*Sheol*, or, hell in the Old Testament,) it is described as a place of darkness to which all the dead go, both the righteous and unrighteous, regardless of the moral decisions they make in life. *Sheol* is also seen as a place of stillness and darkness where a person is cut off from life, and from the Hebrew God.

Though this last point strongly hints to divine punishment for one's sin, most Jewish people believe when the body dies the cycle of life ends. The body returns to the dust of the ground, and the soul dissipates as a vapor. Contributing to this is the fact that only the first five books of the Scriptures, called the Torah, are considered inspired. Most references to Sheol, Hades, and eternal separation from God are found in other books of the Bible, though ample references to the grave are throughout the first five books.

The concept of eternal judgment that Christians believe, and one that follows after death (the Great White Throne Judgment,) is not prevalent in Jewish theology or the minds of Jewish people. Rather, Judaism focuses on the living, being good, and performing acts of charity. At its core, it is concerned with the well-being of humanity.

1. A story is found in the Talmud that is often told when someone is to summarize the essence of Judaism: During the first century B.C.E. a great rabbi named Hillel was asked, to sum up, Judaism while standing on one foot. He replied: *"Certainly! What is hateful to you, do not do to your neighbor. That is the Torah. The rest is commentary, now go and study."* (Talmud Shabbat 31A)

2. This belief is dominant amongst most all sects of Judaism. Because they see no eternal destination based on a personal relationship with God, and how one lived, the following sad concept is derived from the Psalms: *"Death is tragic because it deprives us of the ability to continue to serve our Master."* As the Psalmist wrote it: *"the dead praise, not the Lord, neither any that go down into silence"* (Psalm 116:17).

> **The *Olam Ha Ba* Exception:** There seems to be some exception when it comes to the Orthodox. The Hebrew term "*Olam Ha Ba*" comes into focus, meaning, "the world to come" in Hebrew. Early rabbinic texts describe *Olam Ha Ba* as a physical realm that will exist at the end-of-days after the Messiah has come, and God has judged both the living and the dead. The righteous dead will be resurrected in order to enjoy a second life in *Olam Ha Ba*.
>
> There is also the term Gehenna, which connotes "hell," hidden or unseen; or, the underworld. When the ancient rabbis talk about Gehenna, the question that they are trying to answer is, "How will bad people be dealt with in the afterlife?" After being punished in Gehenna, a soul was considered pure enough to enter Gan Eden, or, Garden of God. Accordingly, they saw Gehenna as a place of punishment for those who led an immoral life.
>
> They also taught that the time a person's soul could remain in Gehenna was limited to twelve months, and the rabbis believed that even at the very Gates of Gehenna a person could repent and avoid punishment. Again, this highlights our earliest remarks about the significant disparities of thought that exist within Judaism.

4. CAN ONE HAVE A PERSONAL RELATIONSHIP WITH GOD?

Following the destruction of the Second Temple in 70 AD by the Romans, Judaism underwent sweeping changes following the cessation of sacrifices in the Temple. With the Temple destroyed, millions of Jews killed, sold into slavery, and thousands more exiled from Jerusalem, a new form of Judaism was needed to rescue it from the brink of extinction.

At the time of Rome's final conquest of Jerusalem, Rabbi Yochanan ben Zakkai, Judaism's spiritual leader at the time, knew for certain resistance was futile. Legend has it, he had his followers secretly carry him out of the city in a coffin, so he could reach the Roman commander and appeal to let him and some of his sages go to Yavneh, a city east of Jerusalem. Given permission, Zakkai established a new institution of learning where matters of law were reorganized. Legal and spiritual rulings began to be disseminated throughout the Diaspora as Jews began to turn to Yavneh for guidance and leadership. His new system was built upon good deeds and the study of Torah. His followers were taught that these elements were more pleasing to God. This early movement ignited a massive overhaul of Judaism that formed the basis for the rabbinic form of Judaism that exists today.

A catastrophic effect of his reforms set the Jewish people on a path away from any concept of a personal relationship with God as the former Prophets had shown them. His followers were taught that these elements were more pleasing to God. This early movement ignited a massive overhaul of Judaism that formed the basis for the rabbinic form of Judaism that exists today.

5. **DO JEWISH PEOPLE BELIEVE IN THE HOLY BIBLE?** Judaism upholds three crowns; the **Crown of Torah,** the **Crown of Priesthood,** and the **Crown of Kingship.** The first connotes our earthly life that is dependent upon Torah; the second speaks to the purpose of the Jewish people and Israel, and the third speaks of the future Messianic Age when King Messiah comes. Christianity places emphasis on both the New and Old, but salvation is mediated through *Yeshua* Jesus as revealed in the sacred New Testament.

This is not the case with Judaism. Right conduct, acts of compassion, caring for the earth, and being good stewards of God's creation is stressed. Judaism does focus on the Mosaic Covenant, which is found in the first five books of the Old Testament (also considered the sacred *Torah,* and consists of Genesis, Exodus, Leviticus, Numbers, and Deuteronomy). The rest of the Old Testament, the *Nevi'im,* (the Prophets,) *K'tubim,* (Writings) and, the Five *Megillot,* (Scrolls,) are held valuable and informative, but they are not considered inspired as the *Torah*. Added to the *Torah* is the *Talmud*, which means "learning and instruction." It consists of two components.

The *Mishnah* is dated 200 CE, which is a written collection of Judaism's Oral Torah, (laws, statutes, and legal interpretations not found in the Five Books of Moses). The second part, the *Gemara*, dated around 500 CE, is a rabbinical analysis of and a commentary on the *Mishna*. But the term "*Talmud*" may refer to either the *Gemara* alone or the *Mishnah* and *Gemara* together.

One final note: According to "Maimonides," the Mishnah was to become the ultimate resource for Jews, Judaism, and Jewish Education. It was intended to provide a complete statement of the Oral Law, so that for a person who mastered first the Written *Torah*, and then the *Mishnah Torah*, there would be no need for any other book.

Judaism's sweeping changes following Yavneh, taught Jews to relate to God through prayers, *Mitzvot* (commandments,) good deeds, (performing *Mitzvah,*) and Charity (*Tzedakah*). These *Mitzvot* are a central part of Judaism still today. So wide-ranging are they that 613 commandments cover all aspects of life. All of them comply with the ethical and ritual teachings of the *Torah*. These can be found in the *Mishna Torah*, (meaning, repetition of the *Torah*). The *Mishna* is the Oral Law, while the *Torah* is the Written Law. To the original question then, the *Torah*, the first five books of the Old Testament, the *Talmud, Mishna*, and *Gemara*, are the holy books of Judaism.

6. **DO JEWISH PEOPLE BELIEVE IN A FUTURE REIGN OF THEIR MESSIAH?** Throughout Jewish history, the Messianic kingdom has been longed for and prayed for. Israel constantly envisioned a time when she would be restored to her former glory, and her people would once again be living in their fullness under the leadership of their Messiah; this is true today as well. The Christian church has longed for the same. But the Christian focus is on such images and realities as the cross, the resurrection, the ascension, and heaven. The Jew sees Jerusalem and Mt. Zion restored, while the Christian sees the "New Jerusalem" coming down out of heaven as seen in Revelation 21:2. While the kingdom of God has permeated Christian teaching, the kingdom of heaven has permeated Judaism.

One distinction from Christianity is over its preconditions. Judaism asserts that to hasten the Messiah's return, we must prepare for the building of the Third Temple. For this reason, the training of priests in the sacrificial system, and the manufacturing of Temple furnishings have been under way in Israel for years. These actions, according to Judaism, will accelerate the return of their Messiah. For Talmudic references of Messiah, see appendix in the back of the book.

7. **DO JEWISH PEOPLE BELIEVE IN ORIGINAL SIN?** 1 Corinthians 15:21-22 states, *"For since by man came death, by man also came the resurrection of the dead. For as in Adam all die, even so in Christ shall all be made alive."* Original Sin remains one of the foundation pillars of Christianity, yet Judaism believes this is unbiblical. Jews believe that one is born into the world with Original Purity and not Original Sin. Judaism recognizes that man is capable of great evil but does not agree with Christianity that man is born with a natural inclination toward sin.

Instead, Judaism focuses on man's human power to choose good over evil. It embraces their belief that God rejoices when a man chooses to be good. The concept of sin entering the world through Adam and Eve, which brought death into the world, is vehemently opposed.

- Judaism also believes that as one man's sin cannot bring death into the world; one man's death cannot bring salvation, or life into the world. Death is seen merely as a natural cycle of life. Rabbis assert that death has existed since the first human beings were created. Hence, man does not die because of their sin, rather, because God made death part of life from the moment of Creation.

MEDITATE UPON THE FOLLOWING:
Offered by Rabbi Myron

1. Some believe in a coming Messiah; some believe in a coming Messianic Age with no specific Messiah.

2. Almost every Jewish person I know is just waiting for you to try and "convert" him/her to a Christian God and Christian culture. A very few may have passed beyond this point and are cautiously curious about the truth of *Yeshua* for themselves. Finally, there are individuals who have gone beyond the veil of "treasonous consideration" of the Messiahship of *Yeshua* and had the courage to risk EVERYTHING for the truth.

3. Most Jews, like most people, are satisfied accepting the perceptions of their faith community and do not venture forth to seek the truth beyond the construction they have cobbled together with their life experience. Until "reality" conflicts with their understanding of it, most people are not open to considering new life paradigms. We must, therefore, not take this as a rejection of the truth but a desire to protect the fragile house of cards that is their understanding of God.

4. Being Jewish is not just a belief in God the Father. In fact, it may EXCLUDE a belief in God. Having said that, it DOES usually include elements of Jewish culture (tradition!), a connection to the land of Israel, and the people of "the book" (belief IN "the Book" or not!). It is not necessary, nor is it advisable, to present a picture of *Yeshua* to such a person that leaves them with the impression that they have to give up any of these facets of their identity to accept the Messiahship of *Yeshua*.

5. Judaism today has evolved into a religion that can be characterized to a great extent as a set of beliefs centered around the denial of *Yeshua* as Messiah. It is not so much focused on the reaching, striving to know God and enhancing a relationship with Him as it is a defense against His Anointed One.

6. Most Jewish people are unfamiliar with their own Holy Scriptures. They are even LESS familiar with and have less confidence in the truth of the *Brit Chadashah*. It will be more profitable to share the truth of *Yeshua* from the *Tenach* (the Older Testament), the Talmud, other sacred sources and the contemporary culture of the first century than the *Brit Chadashah*.

7. The many thousands who came to faith in *Yeshua* during and shortly after His time on earth speak to the power of what was available and acceptable to Jewish people in their time. This will be much more persuasive and more difficult to dismiss than the Newer Testament. Jewish people who hear the Gospel from you are not rejecting you. They are not even, in most cases, rejecting Yeshua. They are just not ready to consider His truth.

Thank you, Rabbi Myron Slobin for your insight

from years of experience in Jewish ministry

NOTES:

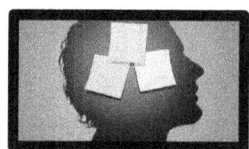

BETRAYED BY A FRIEND: Psalm 41:9 *Even my close friend, someone I trusted, one who shared my bread, has turned against me.* Also, Matthew 26:23; Luke 22:21; John 13:18, 17:12

SMITTEN AND SPAT ON: Isaiah 50:5-7, Matthew 26:67
"The Lord GOD has opened My ear; And I was not disobedient, nor did I turn back. I gave My back to those who strike Me, And My cheeks to those who pluck out the beard; I did not cover My face from humiliation and spitting. For the Lord GOD helps Me, Therefore, I am not disgraced; Therefore, I have set My face like flint, And I know that I will not be ashamed."

FORSAKEN BY GOD: Psalm 22:1, *"My God, my God, why hast thou forsaken me? why art thou so far from helping me, and from the words of my roaring"*

HANDS AND FEET PIERCED: Psalm 22:15-17 *"My strength is dried up like a potsherd, and my tongue cleaves to my jaws; And You lay me in the dust of death. For dogs have surrounded me; A band of evildoers has encompassed me; They pierced my hands and my feet. I can count all my bones. They look, they stare at me."*

JEWISH OBJECTIONS TO CHRISTIAN MESSIANIC CLAIMS

> **Christian Belief:** The Messiah brings an eternal peace between all nations, and all people:[4] Judaism argues that since there is no peace, in fact, there is more war today, Jesus cannot be the prophesied Messiah. Furthermore, *Yeshua* said that his purpose in coming was to bring a sword, and not peace (Matthew 10:34, as referenced above).

> **Christian Belief**: The Messiah will bring about a worldwide conversion of all peoples to ethical Monotheism. Judaism states that since the world still remain steeped in idolatry, *Yeshua* was not the Messiah.

> **Christian Belief:** The Messiah brings about an end to all forms of idolatry (Zechariah. 13:2). Judaism argues that since the world remains steeped in idolatry, *Yeshua* could not have been the Messiah.

> **Christian Belief**: The Messiah brings about a universal recognition of The One True God (Isaiah 11:9). Judaism argues that since the world remains steeped in idolatry, and Christians still believe in a Triune God, *Yeshua* did not fulfill the prophecies spoken of Him.

> **Christian Belief:** The Messiah gathers to Israel all of the twelve tribes (Ezekiel 36:24). Judaism argues that since the Jewish people and the ten tribes remain scattered, *Yeshua* Jesus cannot be the Messiah.

> **Christian Belief:** The Messiah rebuilds the Temple (Isaiah 2:2, Ezekiel 37:26-28). Judaism argues that the Temple has never been built since the Second Temple was destroyed. Therefore, *Yeshua* cannot be the Messiah.

> **Christian Belief**: After the Messiah comes there will be no more famine (Ezekiel 36:29-30). Judaism argues, since famine and poverty still remain, and is even on the rise, *Yeshua* Jesus cannot be the Messiah.

---

[4] Isaiah 2:2-4; Micah 4:1-4; Ezekiel 39:9.

- **Christian Belief**: After the Messiah comes; death will eventually cease (Isaiah 25:8). Judaism argues that since Christianity claims that the Messiah has come is not true because death is still a reality of our times.

- **Christian Belief**: There will be a resurrection following the coming of the Messiah. Judaism[5] argues that the resurrection never occurred. * Although from the New Testament there was a resurrection, Judaism does not recognize the New Testament (Matthew 27:52-53).

- **Christian Belief**: The nations of the earth will help the Jews materially (Isaiah 60:5-6; 60:10). Judaism argues that since more and more nations are promoting anti-Semitism, Israel is still alone, and rarely do any nations come to her aid.

---

[5] Isaiah 26:19; Daniel 12:2; Ezekiel 37:12-13; Isaiah 43:5-

JEWISH HISTORY

History also sheds light on the construct of Messianic Jewish belief in *Yeshua*. Though the early Jewish community yearned to be liberated from Rome's might and pagan life culture, expectations were for a Judah Maccabee type to come and smash the oppressive nations universally, restoring Israel to her former glory. There were no expectations for the Jewish Messiah to fit the Jewish model of *Yeshua's* ministry and style. *Yeshua* claiming to come from the Father confounded the experts! A humble servant who washed His disciples' feet was unfit for their expectations. It was unacceptable when *Yeshua* taught people to turn the other cheek[vi], and the poor and oppressed were called blessed."[vii]

More fundamental, the conflict in what Scripture portrays as Maschiach ben David, (son of David, a kingly figure) and Maschiach ben Joseph, (son of Joseph, a suffering servant,) was difficult to reconcile in one person. Jewish leaders found it difficult to see both figures bringing about a two-part *Tikkun Olam*, repair of the world)[viii] This historical "double Messiah" theory is prevalent still today. Although the Jewish people widely recognize the closeness of the Messiah, a two-thousand-year-old error is about to be made once again.

Double Messiah Theory and the Third Temple: Upon Yeshua's first advent, He came according to what the Talmud refers to as, the "leper scholar."[6] Ironically, He arrived at the exact time in history that was prophesied for this suffering servant, the Son of Joseph, or, Mashiach ben Yosef (Joseph) as noted. Today, Judaism is still waiting for what the Talmud describes as, the "leper scholar." However, according to the book of Revelation, we believe He will return on a white horse as Mashiach ben David, bringing the armies of Heaven with Him. [ix] Here is the most accurate portrayal of the *Leper Scholar* from

---

[6] Sanhedrin 98b

Isaiah 53:3, which was fulfilled two thousand years ago, *"He was despised and rejected by mankind, a man of suffering, and familiar with pain. Like one from whom people hide their face he was despised, and we held him in low esteem."* As already noted, a two-thousand-year-old mistake is going to occur again.

WHY JEWISH PEOPLE DO NOT BELIEVE IN JESUS

For 2,000 years Jews have rejected the Christian idea of Jesus as Messiah. Why?

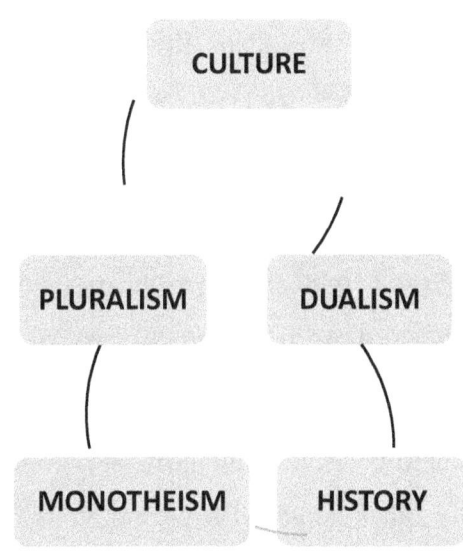

The reason, or more accurately, reasons, that Jewish people do not believe in Jesus is influenced by, **Culture, History, Theology, Pluralism, Dualism,** and **Monotheism.** To one degree or another each one of these influence a cross section of Judaism when it comes to faith in Messiah. We discover something more complicated than mere Romans 10:9, *"If you declare with your mouth that Yeshua is Lord and believe in your heart that God raised Him from the dead, you shall be saved."*

Hence, we discover something more complicated than mere Romans 10:9, If you declare with your mouth, *"Jesus is Lord," and believe in your heart that God raised him from the dead, you will be saved."*

Although the same supernatural work is required for everyone, these three obstacles encumber the path for the Jew. Our aim here is to empower the reader with a greater grasp on how to witness the truth of the Gospel to the Lost Sheep of Israel, given the context of these three areas: **Culture, Theology**, and **History.**

[CULTURE]

For Jewish people to believe in *Yeshua* as the Jewish Messiah, is something that Judaism struggles with to this day. Jewish belief in *Yeshua* has historically represented a contradiction of the very essence of Judaism. Simply, it's not Jewish to believe in Jesus, the Jewish Messiah. Although *Yeshua* (Jesus Hebrew name) was Jewish in every way, these two principles have been in opposition to one another for centuries. Judaism asserts that any belief other than the belief in Jesus is acceptable. This means that a Jewish person can be a practicing Buddhist, Hindu, New Age Philosopher, even an Atheist, and remain wholly Jewish in the eyes of the Jewish community. It seems that only the belief in *Yeshua* forms this historical divide that separates a Jewish believer from the Jewish community. So deeply opposed is Judaism to this concept, some Orthodox Jewish families will actually have a ritualistic funeral deeming the person dead, called, sitting *shiva*. This is a 7-day mourning period that is practiced when a Jewish person dies.

Clearly, what awaits a Jewish person should they receive their Messiah comes wholesale rejection from their Rabbis, Jewish friends, and family. The entire social fabric of their lives is torn apart. Imagine being disowned and considered dead by your parents, siblings and your entire community for receiving Christ. When a Jewish person considers Jesus he or she must weigh the decision carefully before choosing *Yeshua* as his/her Messiah.

The good news, however, is *The Good News*. What I mean to say is. It is still the most powerful and enduring truth that transforms a Jewish person as any other non-Jewish person. It is not uncommon when a Jewish person comes to faith, that a powerful and dramatic encounter with God is experienced. This provides the supernatural strength of the Holy Spirit to help them through some of these early difficulties. For the Jew then, cultural pressures abound, and Messianic faith for the Jew poses real and formidable obstacles. But as more and more Jewish people come to faith, this wall becomes easier to overcome; familiarity with other Jewish people coming to faith fosters credibility in Jewish Messianic faith.

[PLURALISM]

Today, many Jewish people view the belief in God differently than in past periods of history. The Post-modern age[x], for instance, has in large part redefined religious thought in Judaism as well as Christianity. The post-modern Jew, excluding the Orthodox and Conservative, does not know whether he or she even believes in God. Radical pluralism, a characteristic of postmodernism, poses great difficulties to come to a consensus on the very doctrine of God. This is because pluralism eradicates absolutes, replaces it with self, and values inner thought and exploration.

For many Jews "spirituality" begins from within that is derived from one's individual perception of the universe coupled with a perspective of one's own existence in the context of that universe. For this, the kind of spirituality presented in the New Testament is unfit for this new thought. Jews like to think of God as being outside of creation, something that is more as a life force, or, energy flowing in and through creation. If there were anything that a Jew could call "God," it would be a Unity, or, a Oneness, which is something that pervades all things, and, is found by turning inside oneself. For this reason, many Jewish people are Agnostic.

Ironically, Christianity also requires one to turn inside. Although its purpose is radically different, an individual is invited to discover one's own sin and inner darkness. Christianity upholds the belief, that sin remains the human barrier between God and man, and each person must come to this discovery. Once this is discovered, only then does one turn outward, and upward, to receive forgiveness of their sins. Only then does God restore right perspective along with the right perception of the universe; both are brought back into alignment with God. This is the truest form of *Tikkun O'lam* (repair of the world).

[MONOTHEISM]

A great challenge to Messianic faith is Judaism's foundation of Monotheism, the belief that there is only one God. For thousands of years, Judaism has upheld a monotheistic faith, the belief in the One True God of Abraham, Isaiah, and Jacob. Two thousand years ago, upon Messiah's arrival, this historic Jewish monotheism was challenged to its core when the concept and doctrine of One God operating in three persons (the Trinity) were introduced. How Jews perceive the Trinity is vastly different than Christians. Two thousand years ago, and even in our modern day, *Yeshua* claiming to come from the Father was blasphemy and historically, a source of disdain. Still, many Post-Modern Jews are challenging 4,000-year-old Monotheism in their own way and are coming from Pluralism and Dualism. From a true philosophical monism, the doctrine that only one supreme being exists, is in itself a rejection of any dualism and is the only doctrine that can satisfy many postmodern Jews.

[DUALISM]

Dualism implies that there are two moral opposites at work; two forces independent of any interpretation of what might be "moral," and "independent" of how these may be represented. This again is a grave error and a contradiction of both Christianity and Judaism. Judeo-Christian Monotheism, coupled with the belief in *Yeshua* the Messiah, is the only means to restore balance in one's life. God is God, and this God is over all other gods! Although this is a brief sweep of Jewish objections to New Covenant faith, one can see the layers of Jewish objection in the context of Jewish culture, both historically as well as in our modern day.

NOTES:

SECTION VII

UNDERSTANDING JEWISH ESCHATOLOGY, HISTORY, CULTURE, THEOLOGY:

SUPPLEMENTAL STUDY: NINE SECTS OF JUDAISM:

 Understanding how the Jewish people see the end times is an important piece to presenting the end of days given a New Testament perspective. Jewish eschatology (the study of the last days) has much in common with respect to the Messianic Kingdom. But diverse points exist when it comes to the final judgment, original sin, and the final resting place of the human soul.

In this section we provide an overview of Jewish history, culture and theology as it offers insight into how we can better prepare for Jewish evangelism. Numerous sects exist within Judaism that can hinder our understanding of the Jewish people. Each one has divergent points from the traditional understanding of the Torah.

UNDERSTANDING JEWISH ESCHATOLOGY, HISTORY, CULTURE, AND THEOLOGY

"Often, the 'glorious message' of the church is not its rejection of Jewish people, but its complete rejection of all things Jewish."

- *Felix Halpern*

In Jewish understanding of the last days, the term "*Mashiach*," or "Messiah," commonly referred to a future Jewish King from the Davidic line, who was to rule the Jewish people during the Messianic Age; the Messiah is often referred to as "King Messiah." According to Hebrew Orthodox views, He should be descended from his father through the line of King David and will gather the Jews back into the land of Israel. Then He will usher in an era of peace and re-build the Third Temple. This will fulfill the role of Mashiach ben David, and simultaneously, fulfill the role of Mashiach ben Yosef (Joseph.) The Talmud demonstrates this conflict when it describes the future return of the Messiah extensively in a portion of the

Talmud, Sanhedrin 98a–99a. Described, is a period of freedom and peace that the Jews, and the nations will experience together. Here are some examples to consider:

- ✡ R. Johanan said when you see a generation ever dwindling, hope for him [the Messiah], as it is written, *"And the afflicted people thou wilt save."*[xi] R. Johanan said, when thou see a generation overwhelmed by many troubles as by a river, await him, as it is written, *"When the enemy shall come in like a flood, the Spirit of the Lord shall lift up a standard against him;"* which is followed by, *"And the Redeemer shall come to Zion."*

- ✡ R. Johanan also said the son of David would come only in a generation that is either altogether righteous or altogether wicked.[7] *in a generation that is altogether righteous,* — as it is written, "Thy people also shall be all righteous: they shall inherit the land forever." *Or altogether wicked,* — as it is written, *"And he saw that there was no man, and wondered that there was no intercessor;"* and it is [elsewhere] written, *"For mine own sake, even for mine own sake, will I do it."*

- ✡ The Talmud also relates many stories about the Messiah, some of which are from famous Talmudic rabbis that have claimed to have personal visitations from <u>Elijah the Prophet</u>. For example, R. Joshua b. Levi met <u>Elijah</u> standing by the entrance of R. Simeon b. Yohai's tomb. He asked him: "Have I a portion in the world to come?" He replied, "if this Master desires it." R. Joshua b. Levi said, "I saw two, but heard the voice of a third."

    He Then asked him, "When will the Messiah come?" — "Go and ask him himself," was his reply. "Where is he sitting?" — "At the entrance." "And by what sign may I recognize him?" — "He is sitting among the poor lepers: all

---

[7] Talmud Sanhedrin 98a

of them untie [them] all at once, and re-bandage them together, whereas he unties and bandages each separately, [before treating the next], thinking, should I be wanted, [it being time for my appearance as the Messiah] I must not be delayed [through having to bandage a number of sores]." So, he went to him and greeted him, saying, "Peace upon thee, Master and Teacher." "Peace upon thee, O son of Levi," he replied. "When wilt thou come, Master?" asked he. "Today," was his answer. On his returning to Elijah, the latter enquired, "What did he say to thee?" — "peace upon thee, O son of Levi," he answered. Thereupon he [Elijah] observed, "He thereby assured thee and thy father of [a portion in] the world to come." "He spoke falsely to me," he rejoined, "stating that he would come today, but has not." He [Elijah] answered him, "This is what he said to thee, To-day if ye will listen to his voice."[8]

[CHRISTIAN HISTORY]

To study the institutional church, is to expose numerous times in her history when Jewish and Christian relations were breached. Something that is easily determined, was a new Gentile expression apart from Judaism. This was imperative for those who wanted a new Roman foundation, and perhaps more, one void of all its former Jewish forms, practices, and traditions. Compounding the spirit and tone of the early Christian era, early church fathers misinterpreted key events that spawned an anti-Jewish atmosphere.

One can site the destruction of the Temple, which the early church fathers saw as God's rejection of His people. Additionally, the idea of holding the Jewish people responsible for Christ's death, coupled with Constantine's many anti-Jewish edicts and rulings, fostered a legacy of Jewish hate that contributed greatly to erected long standing walls of separation between the Jew and Gentile, Judaism and Christianity.

---

[8] Talmud Sanhedrin 98a

In other words, history reveals that the split between the Jew and the Gentile[xii], the church from its Jewish root, began early. It occurred in a crucible of cultural and ecclesiastical revolution. Also, it occurred in a course over a period of time. But unmistakably, it was cataclysmic to God's design. Soon patterns of thinking emerged that germinated anti-Jewish theologies, producing generations of bias against Jews. Of course, the Jewish people, being the victims of these changes, developed an abiding fear that was coupled with hostility and distrust towards Christianity.

While false theologies such as "replacement," "displacement," "supersessionism," inculcated seminaries and denominations, generations of Christians lost a prophetic understanding of God's plan for the Jewish people. The notion that Israel and the Jew were the rejected of God was reinforced by a system of interpretive thought that was highly flawed and based upon anti-Semitism. Now, following centuries of misunderstanding, one can see how such terms as **Christ, church, crusade, conversion,** and **cross**, formed its own crown of thorns for Jewish people. History branded Christianity as a religion that brought much anti-Semitism and suffering.

[JEWS AND THE ROMAN WORLD]

As early as the Roman world of Messiah two thousand years ago, there was a growing hostility between the Jewish people and the culture of the Roman world. This is brought to light in the words of Cicero, (106-43 BCE) who was a politician and philosopher before the destruction of the second temple: "Even while Jerusalem was still standing the Jews were at peace with us, the practice of their sacred rites, however, were at variance with the glory of our empire, the dignity of our name."

Just as Cicero noted, a variance between Judaism and the Roman Empire in the years BCE, when it comes to Roman Christianity and the following centuries, was an empire religion. This was in direct opposition to the Messianic type rule that Jews longed for. Consequently, Jews who wanted to embrace *Yeshua* (and many did for cultural, political, and economic reasons) had to renounce their Jewish identity and turn from the faith of their biblical forefathers. Jews were forced to convert to a Gentile form of faith.

In his book *Restoring the Jewishness of the Gospel*, David Stern notes that the Jews were required to swear to and sign the following: "I renounce all customs, rites, legalisms, unleavened breads, sacrifices of lambs of the Hebrews, and all the other Feasts of the Hebrews, sacrifices, prayers, aspersions, purifications, sanctifications, propitiations, feasts, new moons, Sabbaths, superstitions, hymns, chants, observances, synagogues, the food, and drink of the Hebrews.

They had to renounce absolutely everything Jewish, every law, rite, and custom— if afterwards, I shall wish to deny and return to Jewish superstitions, or shall be found eating with Jews, or feasting with them, or secretly conversing and condemning the Christian religion instead of openly confuting them and condemning their vain faith, then let the trembling of Cain and the leprosy of Gehazi cleave to me, as well as the legal punishments to which I acknowledge myself liable. And may I be an anathema in the world to come, and my soul be set down with Satan and the devils." Hence, many obstacles were thrown in the path of a Jewish person considering faith in *Yeshua* as the Messiah. A Jewish saying accurately portrays both Israel and the Jewish people.

> **"Israel is likened to a man traveling on the road when he encountered a wolf and escaped from it, and he went along relating the affair of a wolf. He then encountered a lion and escaped from it and went along relating the affair of the lion. He then encountered a snake, escaped from it, after that he forgot the two previous incidents and went along relating the affair of the snake. So, it is with Israel; the present troubles cause them to forget the earlier one."[9]**

The above saying speaks of the Jew as it does with Israel. Satan has long sought to destroy the Jew and infect both society and Christendom with anti-Semitism.

---

[9] Berakoth 13a

[ISRAEL AND THE NATIONS]

An accurate relationship is described in Scripture when it comes to Israel's relationship to the nations. One that is seen with her historical enemy Aram (Syria), can be likened to water and fire. In a prophecy concerning Damascus, it states, *"Woe to the roar of the many nations who are tumultuous as the seas roar."*[10]

In Obadiah, the Jewish people are compared to fire, "The House of Yaakov be fire"[xiii] This simple analogy points to a well-known biblical fact: The Jewish people were to be the fire and light to the world and, accordingly, spread the light of the One True God and His kingdom principles. However, like water that extinguishes the fire, nations have made countless attempts to smother the Jew. This may seem at first as a harsh indictment, but one cannot truly receive a heart for the Jewish people if we do not understand their historical suffering; much persecution came in the form of a Christian missions. This history branded Christianity as anti-Semitic.

[RELIGION OF JEWISH HATE]

As noted, Christianity came to be seen as a religion of Jewish hate. A persecutory history came in the name of Jesus and, tragically, under the sign of the Cross. Judaism, of course, perceived no similitude or attraction to Christianity, even though Judaism was the foundation of Christianity. To the Jewish people then, Christianity came to embody a belief, culture, and history that repelled Jews. The Christian sacraments of early Catholicism, its rituals, worship of saints, and her graven images of these saints, were in direct conflict with the Torah of Judaism. [xiv] Of course, the Catholic Church and its edicts that ensued shaped much of this persecutory history. Nevertheless, Christianity in the eyes of historical Judaism became framed in this context. And for this reason, one cannot separate this Christian history from Jewish history when desiring to know why Jewish people reject the belief in Jesus. Today, however, large portions of the Christian body are finding new opportunities to understand these errors of history, and Jewish people are considering faith in the Jewish Messiah in a new light.

---

[10] *Yeshayahu* – Isaiah 17:12)

[JEWISH THEOLOGY]

Although Judaism asserts that Yeshua Jesus did not fulfill the Messianic prophecies, they claim the Scriptures pointing to Him have been mistranslated. *Yeshua* during his time on earth, and His manner of ministry, according to Judaism, did not fulfill the personal qualifications of the Messiah. Perhaps the most important obstacle to this belief is the fact that Jewish belief in *Yeshua* must have a national revelation and redemption. This has been prevalent since the coming of Messiah two thousand years ago, and up to our present day and into the future.

The point being made here is truly unique from other religions, especially Christianity. Judaism looks at Messianic fulfillments in very different ways than Christians. Yet the Jewish basis for interpretation remains the foundation for both their acceptance in the future and also our present day. What we are describing here is the general view from the perspective of the Rabbis throughout the whole of Judaism and, generally, in Orthodox and Conservative streams. When it comes to revelation, and personal experiences in the context of Messianic anticipation, a national revelation of the Messiah is essential for Jewish fulfillments of Messiah for the following reasons:

According to Judaism, no individual experience or account of a miracle is enough to validate Messianic claims. The Damascus road experience by the Apostle Paul for instance, [xv] is in deep conflict with Judaism. Rabbis state first that the Bible clearly shows that God allows false miracles as well. So, who is to determine which one is from God, and which one is counterfeit. It is important than to remain fixed in the Torah and to obey God and God alone (Deuteronomy 13:4). Judaism asserts that the Israelites believed in Moses, not because of any miracles. The Revelation at Mount Sinai for example, was experienced by all—they all saw and heard with their own eyes and ears, and it was not upon the testimony of one or another; *"Face to face, God spoke with you."*

When it comes to Messiah's coming, Rabbis assert that it involves every man, woman, and child, witnessing it with their eyes and ears as it took place at Mount Sinai 3,300 years ago. This goes back to the principle of a national revelation. This national revelation test, combined with a national return of Israel test, and the restored Messianic order, all converge upon the return of the Messiah, according to Judaism. This of course is correct in the context of the millennial kingdom. But the timing and sequence are incorrect in Jewish thinking. The culmination of this age is predicated upon all Israel coming to a national re-generation, and this is true. [xvi]Here are some passages to consider. In Matthew 23:39; Luke 13:35 it states, *"for I tell you, you will not see me again until you say, 'Blessed is he who comes in the name of the Lord."*

- Psalm 118:26, *"Bless is he who comes in the name of the Lord From the house of the Lord we bless You."*
- Zechariah 12:10, *"And I will pour out on the house of David and the inhabitants of Jerusalem a spirit of grace and supplication. They will look on me, the one they have pierced, and they will mourn for Him as one mourns for an only child and grieve bitterly for Him as one grieves for a firstborn son."*
- Hosea 5:15, *"Then I will return to my lair until they have borne their guilt and seek my face – in their misery they will earnestly seek me."*

All of the preceding passages speak about a national regeneration that will take place upon the return of the Lord. But this return follows a simultaneous recognition of *Yeshua*. Tragically, Judaism could not accept their humble servant King two thousand years ago, because they could not understand the two-part plan of world redemption that would take place. *Yeshua* did fulfill the role as the suffering son of Joseph, and He is now returning as the son of King David. Then and only then will there be a national revitalization of Israel.

[JEWISH MESSIANISM]

In the following, we offer a brief list of Jewish tenets of Messianic belief that Judaism claims remain unfulfilled. Though the following is only a brief survey of a comprehensive study, Judaism holds numerous points of Messianism in objection that covers three specific areas;

History, Culture, and **Theology.** As each area is reviewed one becomes more effective in fielding Jewish objections against Messianic belief.

- Judaism claims that *Yeshua* Jesus must be descended from the house of King David. Judaism claims *Yeshua* was not. [xvii]

- Judaism claims that *Yeshua* cannot be God and man at the same time. Yet, in the book of John, this is exactly descriptive of the *Messiah*. In the beginning was the Word, and the Word was with God, and the Word was God, and the Word was made flesh and dwelt among us.

- Judaism asserts that *Yeshua* was to bring peace to the world. Rabbis state that since we have war more than ever, it proves *Yeshua* was not the Messiah. [xviii]

- Judaism asserts that *Messiah* will gather all Jews back to Israel, and since the Jewish people remain scattered, *Yeshua* Jesus was not the Messiah.

- Judaism asserts that *Yeshua* will rebuild the ancient Temple in Jerusalem. Rabbi's state that since the Temple has not been rebuilt, *Yeshua* was not the Messiah.

- Judaism asserts that *Yeshua* will unite humanity in the worship of the Jewish God and Torah observance. Rabbis state that since this has not occurred, *Yeshua* was not the Messiah.

SUPPLEMENTAL STUDY:

NINE SECTS OF JUDAISM

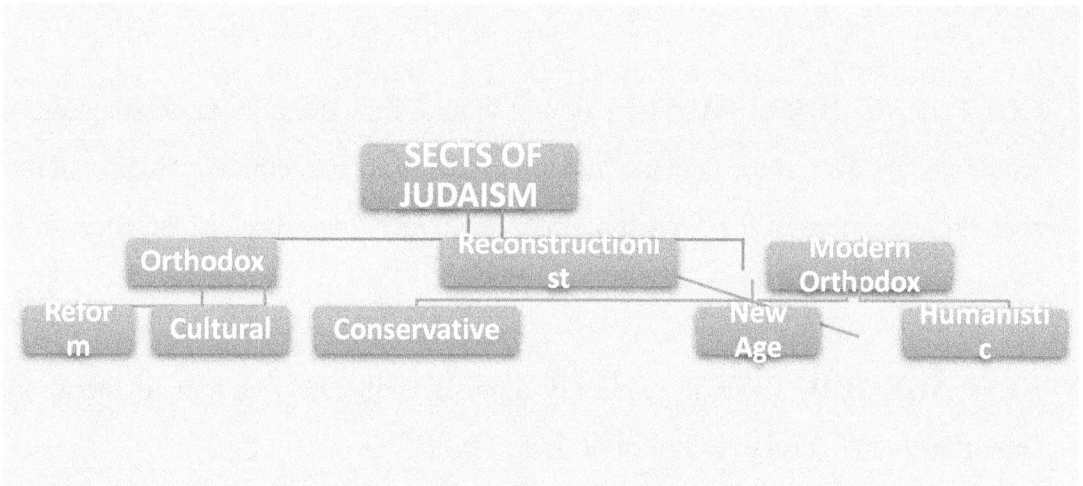

✡ **ULTRA-ORTHODOX / HAREDI:** This stream of Judaism maintains a steadfast adherence to Jewish religious law by segregating itself from modern society. According to Haredi Jews, authentic Jews believe God wrote the Torah, strictly observe Jewish Law *(halacha)*, and refuses to modify Judaism to meet contemporary needs. The word Haredi is derived from the Hebrew word for fear *(harada)* and can be interpreted as, "One who trembles in awe of God" (Isaiah 66:2,5).

✡ **ORTHODOX JUDAISM:** Maintains the historical understanding of Jewish identity. A Jew is someone who was born to a Jewish mother or who converts to Judaism in accordance with Jewish law and tradition.

✡ **MODERN ORTHODOX:** Attempts to synthesize Jewish values and the observance of Jewish law with the secular, modern world.

✡ **CONSERVATIVE JUDAISM:** Highly prevalent in North America, and seeks to preserve Jewish tradition and ritual, but has a more flexible approach to the interpretation of the law than Orthodox Judaism.

- ✡ **REFORM JUDAISM:** Asserts that Jewish traditions should be modernized and integrated into Western culture. This means that many branches of Reform Judaism hold that the Jewish law should undergo a process of critical evaluation and renewal.

- ✡ **CULTURAL JUDAISM:** Garners individual thought and understanding. Its relation to Judaism is through the history, civilization, and ethical values, and those shared experiences of the Jewish people: languages, literature, art, science, dance, music, food, and, celebrations.

- ✡ **NEW AGE JUDAISM:** Is explicitly atheistic with the freedom to incorporate certain elements foreign to Rabbinic Judaism.

- ✡ **HUMANISTIC JUDAISM:** Embraces a human-centered philosophy, which combines rational thinking with a deep connection to the Jewish people and their culture.

- ✡ **RECONSTRUCTIONIST JUDAISM:** This is the foundation for a growing number of Jewish Communities and is a modern American-based Jewish movement originally born from the reforms and ideas of Mordecai Kaplan (1881–183). This movement views *Judaism* as a progressively evolving civilization.

1. Of the Nine Sects of Judaism, which ones are the most difficult to reach, and why?

2. Can you recognize which group or groups best depict the Jewish communities in your area? Ultra-Orthodox _____ Orthodox _____ Modern Orthodox _____ Reform _____ Cultural _____ Conservative _____ New Age _____ Humanistic _____ Reconstructionist _____.

3. Can you think of 3 unique obstacles that each one present in reaching Jewish people?

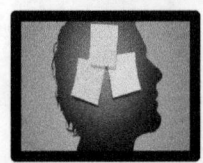

MORE MESSIANIC PROPHECIES

1	Genesis 3:15	Matthew 1:20 Galatians 4:4	
2	Messiah would be born in Bethlehem.	Micah 5:2	Matthew 2:1 Luke 2:4-6
3	Messiah would be born of a virgin.	Isaiah 7:14	Matthew 1:22-23 Luke 1:26-31
4	Messiah would come from the line of Abraham.	Genesis 12:3 Genesis 22:18	Matthew 1:1 Romans 9:5
5	Messiah would be a descendant of Isaac.	Genesis 17:19 Genesis 21:12	Luke 3:34
6	Messiah would be a descendant of Jacob.	Numbers 24:17	Matthew 1:2
7	Messiah would come from the tribe of Judah.	Genesis 49:10	Luke 3:33 Hebrews 7:14
8	Messiah would be heir to King David's throne.	2 Samuel 7:12-13 Isaiah 9:7	Luke 1:32-33 Romans 1:3
9	Messiah's throne will be anointed and eternal.	Psalm 45:6-7 Daniel 2:44	Luke 1:33 Hebrews 1:8-12
10	Messiah would be called Immanuel.	Isaiah 7:14	Matthew 1:23
11	Messiah would spend a season in Egypt.	Hosea 11:1	Matthew 2:14-15
12	A massacre of children would happen at Messiah's birthplace.	Jeremiah 31:15	Matthew 2:16-18
13	A messenger would prepare the way for Messiah	Isaiah 40:3-5	Luke 3:3-6
14	Messiah would be rejected by his own people.	Psalm 69:8 Isaiah 53:3	John 1:11 John 7:5
15	Messiah would be a prophet.	Deuteronomy 18:15	Acts 3:20-22
16	Messiah would be preceded by Elijah.	Malachi 4:5-6	Matthew 11:13-14
17	Messiah would be declared the Son of God.	Psalm 2:7	Matthew 3:16-17
18	Messiah would be called a Nazarene.	Isaiah 11:1	Matthew 2:23
19	Messiah would bring light to Galilee.	Isaiah 9:1-2	Matthew 4:13-16
20	Messiah would speak in parables.	Psalm 78:2-4 Isaiah 6:9-10	Matthew 13:10-15, 34-35

#	Prophecy	OT Reference	NT Fulfillment
21	Messiah would be sent to heal the brokenhearted.	Isaiah 61:1-2	Luke 4:18-19
22	Messiah would be a priest after the order of Melchizedek.	Psalm 110:4	Hebrews 5:5-6
23	Messiah would be called King.	Psalm 2:6 Zechariah 9:9	Matthew 27:37 Mark 11:7-11
24	Messiah would be praised by little children.	Psalm 8:2	Matthew 21:16
25	Messiah would be betrayed.	Psalm 41:9 Zechariah 11:12-13	Luke 22:47-48 Matthew 26:14-16
26	Messiah's price money would be used to buy a potter's field.	Zechariah 11:12-13	Matthew 27:9-10
27	Messiah would be falsely accused.	Psalm 35:11	Mark 14:57-58
28	Messiah would be silent before his accusers.	Isaiah 53:7	Mark 15:4-5
29	Messiah would be spat upon and struck.	Isaiah 50:6	Matthew 26:67
30	Messiah would be hated without cause.	Psalm 35:19 Psalm 69:4	John 15:24-25
31	Messiah would be crucified with criminals.	Isaiah 53:12	Matthew 27:38 Mark 15:27-28
32	Messiah would be given vinegar to drink.	Psalm 69:21	Matthew 27:34 John 19:28-30
33	Messiah's hands and feet would be pierced.	Psalm 22:16 Zechariah 12:10	John 20:25-27
34	Messiah would be mocked and ridiculed.	Psalm 22:7-8	Luke 23:35
35	Soldiers would gamble for Messiah's garments.	Psalm 22:18	Luke 23:34 Matthew 27:35-36
36	Messiah's bones would not be broken.	Exodus 12:46 Psalm 34:20	John 19:33-36
37	Messiah would be forsaken by God.	Psalm 22:1	Matthew 27:46
38	Messiah would pray for his enemies.	Psalm 109:4	Luke 23:34
39	Soldiers would pierce Messiah's side.	Zechariah 12:10	John 19:34
40	Messiah would be buried with the rich.	Isaiah 53:9	Matthew 27:57-60
41	Messiah would resurrect from the dead.	Psalm 16:10 Psalm 49:15	Matthew 28:2-7 Acts 2:22-32
42	Messiah would ascend to heaven.	Psalm 24:7-10	Mark 16:19 Luke 24:51
43	Messiah would be seated at God's right hand.	Psalm 68:18 Psalm 110:1	Mark 16:19 Matthew 22:44
44	Messiah would be a sacrifice for sin.	Isaiah 53:5-12	Romans 5:6-8

SECTION VIII

MESSIANIC KINGDOM

JEWISH ELECTION AND CALLING

JEWISH ELECTION AND THE KINGDOM

KINGDOM STUDY I

KINGDOM STUDY II

JEWISH ELECTION AND THE KINGDOM

MESSIANIC KINGDOM

- FEASTS RESTORED: ZECHARIAH 14:18
- 12 JEWISH APOSTLES RETURN TO RULE OVER THE 12 TRIBES OF ISRAEL: MATTHEW 19:28
- IRREVOCABLE CALL OF THE JEWISH PEOPLE IS FINALLY COMPLETED: ROMANS 11:29
- GREAT PATRIARCHS RETURN: MATTHEW 8:11; LUKE 13:29
- FORMER KING DAVID RETURNS AS PRINCE OVER ISRAEL: EZEKIEL 37:24-25, HOSEA 3:4-5

JERUSALEM WILL BE THE CENTER OF WORSHIP: ISAIAH 2:2; ZECHARIAH 14:16

- GREAT PATRIARCHS RETURN: MATTHEW 8:11; LUKE 13:29
- FORMER KING DAVID RETURNS AS PRINCE OVER ISRAEL: EZEKIEL 37:24-25, HOSEA 3:4-5
- ISRAEL'S FINAL RETURN AND GLORY: DEUTERONOMY 28:13

Given the chart on the previous page, and knowing the importance of the future kingdom, the difference between the kingdom of God and the kingdom of heaven can shed proper light upon Jewish election along with their irrevocable calling. One might wonder what purpose this study has for Jewish evangelism.

Well, understanding the difference between the "Kingdom of Heaven" and the "Kingdom of God," exposes God's complete timeline of prophetic history: the past, present, and future. And without a proper distinction between the two, the Jewish people and Israel suffer again from theologies and interpretative reasoning, where they once again lose their purpose and design. Reaching Jewish people for Christ is one thing; knowing their God-given prophetic destiny is another.

There is no dispute that Israel rejected the Messiah when He first came. At the time, the religious rulers were looking for a political Messiah King who would make Israel the ruling kingdom of the world (Jeremiah. 23:5, Psalms. 48:2). They were also expecting a warrior leader rather than a servant leader, humble, and willing to turn the other cheek. They were desperate to be delivered from the military might of Rome along with the rest of the heathen influences at the time. But due to their hardened hearts and their legalistic and ritualistic zeal, they were blind to their need for a spiritual deliverance and the true righteousness of God, which must come from a transformation of the heart. That is what led them to ask this of Jesus:

"And when he was demanded of the Pharisees when the kingdom of God should come, he answered them and said, the kingdom of God cometh not with observation: Neither shall they say, Lo here! or, lo there! for, behold, the kingdom of God is within you." (Luke 17:20-21 KJV).

On another occasion when *Yeshua* was asked a similar question his answer was different: *Jesus said, "My kingdom is not of this world. If it were, my servants would fight to prevent my arrest by the Jewish leaders. But **now** my kingdom is from another place."* John 18:36 NIV) In the second passage the word "now" is not speaking about the spiritual Kingdom of God (within the heart of the redeemed), but of a literal political Kingdom yet to come on this Earth. If it was His servants would fight for it. From the International Standard Version, here is the same verse; *'Jesus answered, "My kingdom does not belong to this world. If my kingdom belonged to this world, my servants would fight to keep me from being handed over to the Jewish leaders. But for now, my kingdom is not from here."*

It is important to note that numerous translations have removed the word "now" because many are A millennial in position. In other words, they do not accept the literal return of *Yeshua* to reign on the Earth for a thousand years as foretold in in the book of Revelation 20:4-6. Hence when *Yeshua* was speaking to His Jewish disciples they knew what He was speaking of and they pointedly asked when the literal Kingdom would come:

"When they, therefore, were come together, they asked of him, saying, Lord, wilt thou at this time restore again the kingdom to Israel? And he said unto them; it is not for you to know the times or the seasons, which the Father hath put in his own power. But ye shall receive power, after that the Holy Ghost comes upon you: and ye shall be witnesses unto me both in Jerusalem, and in all Judaea, and in Samaria, and unto the uttermost part of the earth." (Acts 1:6-8 KJV)

The disciples were clearly asking about a literal Kingdom, and the Lord says it is not for them to know the time when that literal Kingdom (the Kingdom of Heaven) will take place. Until that time, the disciples were given the power to preach the Kingdom of God—righteousness through faith in the risen Savior who will return to earth one day and rule over the whole earth from Jerusalem. This establishes the basis for understanding the difference between the "Kingdom of God," and the "Kingdom of Heaven." Also, a true prophetic picture is drawn regarding Israel's future as well as the Jewish people. Let's break this down further.

KINGDOM STUDY OUTLINE I
KINGDOM OF GOD / KINGDOM OF HEAVEN

- ***Yeshua's had a dualistic message: The "Kingdom of God," and the "Kingdom of Heaven."*** To the Jews, and the heirs of the promised political Kingdom, the Lord preached the Gospel of the "Kingdom of Heaven" – This was a literal physical Kingdom soon to come: *"From that time Jesus began to preach, and to say, Repent: for the kingdom of heaven is at hand."* (Matthew 4:17 KJV)

- To the Jews and the entire Gentile world, Yeshua preached the coming *"Kingdom of God"* - righteousness and holiness*: "Now after that John was put in prison, Jesus came into Galilee, preaching the gospel of the kingdom of God, and saying, the time is fulfilled, and the kingdom of God is at hand: repent ye, and believe the gospel"* (Mark 1:14 KJV).

- *Yeshua* was preaching about two (2) components of the Kingdom: A political kingdom, the Kingdom of Heaven, and a spiritual kingdom, the Kingdom of God. Both where to take place in the hearts of all people, Jew and Gentile. For this reason, during His brief ministry, Yeshua used the terms "Kingdom of Heaven" and "Kingdom of God" interchangeably. This double reference often takes places in the four Gospels. The result is that many Christians think they are one and the same. *Give thought to which kingdom was established upon Israel's rejection of the Messiah*

- Only until the Second Coming of the Lord when He rules the world for a thousand years on the throne of His father David (His father in the flesh, His human side) at Jerusalem will the Kingdom of Heaven take place. *"Jesus answered., My kingdom is not of this world: if my kingdom were of this world, then would my servant's fight, that I should not be delivered to the Jews: but now is my kingdom not from hence.(* John 18:36 KJV).

 Show in the Scriptures the difference between the terms "Kingdom of Heaven" and "Kingdom of God", the Holy Spirit has put this little nugget of truth within the Gospel of Matthew, *"And from the days of John the Baptist until now the kingdom of heaven suffereth violence, and the violent take it by force."* (Matthew 11:12 KJV). This is a worthy study that opens doors of new understanding regarding the calling and election of Israel. We offer more comments in this manual, but a more in-depth study would serve us well here. But one observation is important. The Kingdom that Israel understood, was God's people living in Jerusalem, under the Headship of the Messiah in the Lord's chosen place from which to rule: *"But I say unto you, swear not at all; neither by heaven; for it is God's throne: Nor by the earth; for it is his footstool: neither by Jerusalem; for it is the city of the great King"*(Matthew 5:34-35 KJV).

✡ **THE MYSTERY KINGDOM: In the two millennia since Israel rejected their King, His Kingdom has been in a MYSTERY form; the Lord *Yeshua is* reigning in the heart of the believer and yet He is seated on the right hand of the Father in the third heaven.** *"[Even] the mystery which hath been hid from ages and from generations, but now is made manifest to his saints: To whom God would make known what [is] the riches of the glory of this mystery among the Gentiles; which is Christ in you, the hope of glory,"*(Colossians 1:26-27 KJV).

- Satan still holds the physical throne over this present world: *"And the devil said unto him, all this power will I give thee, and the glory of them: for that is delivered unto me; and to whomsoever I will I give it. If thou, therefore, wilt worship me, all shall be thine"*(Luke 4:6-7 KJV).

- Although Satan has already lost the war, the final battle for physical Planet earth is yet to come. This is the present status of the Kingdom of Heaven.

- The Apostle Paul said this: *"For I would not, brethren, that ye should be ignorant of this mystery, lest ye should be wise in your own conceits; that blindness in part happens to Israel until the fullness of the Gentiles be come in. And so, all Israel shall be saved: as it is written, there shall come out of Sion the Deliverer, and shall turn away ungodliness from Jacob"* (Romans 11:25-26 KJV).

- We are living in the last days of the blessing to the Gentiles. The Jews are back in the land of Israel although they are still in unbelief about Jesus. Although they are the enemies of the Gospel of Grace by the Lord Jesus Christ, they are still God's people, and He will use the present evil world to chastise them, open their eyes to the truth they rejected, and bring them again to Him.

"As concerning the gospel, they are enemies for your sakes: but as touching the election, they are beloved for the fathers' sakes. For the gifts and calling of God are without repentance. For as ye in times past have not believed God yet have now obtained mercy through their unbelief" (Romans 11:28-30 KJV).

TWO END TIME EVENTS MUST TAKE PLACE BEFORE THE LORDS RETURN:

1. First, there will be some kind of contract among all parties in end of days when it comes to a false peace pact with Jerusalem. This is spoken of by the prophet Daniel: *"Then shall he return into his land with great riches; and his heart shall be against the **holy covenant**, and he shall do exploits, and return to his own land. At the time appointed he shall return, and come toward the south, but it shall not be as the former, or as the latter. For the ships of Chittim shall come against him: therefore, he shall be grieved, and return, and have indignation against the **holy covenant:** so, shall he do; he shall even return and have intelligence with them that forsake the **holy covenant**. And arms shall stand on his part, and they shall pollute the sanctuary of strength, and shall take*

away the daily sacrifice, and they shall place the abomination that market desolate." (Daniel 11:28-31 KJV).

2. Second, a new Temple will be built in Jerusalem in the future! Notice the context above is about the exploits of the coming Antichrist, whom unbelieving Israel and the unbelieving world will welcome as the Messiah. Take note about the "daily sacrifice" and the sanctuary, and the abomination that "maketh desolate." There cannot be a daily sacrifice without a Temple. This is a cross reference to what the Apostle Paul spoke about in 2 Thessalonians.

> *"That ye be not soon shaken in mind, or be troubled, neither by spirit, nor by word, nor by letter as from us, as that the day of Christ is at hand. Let no man deceive you by any means: for that day shall not come, except there comes a falling away first, and that man of sin be revealed, the son of perdition; Who opposeth and exalteth himself above all that is called God, or that is worshipped; so that he as God sitteth in the temple of God, shewing himself that he is God"* (2 Thessalonians. 2:2-4 KJV).

3. The entire theme of the Bible is about the battle over a Kingdom and the rightful ruler of that Kingdom. This goes back before Adam's day. *Remember, the story of the whole Bible from the very beginning until the end is about the spiritual battle for the Kingdom. The eventual triumphant ruler of that Kingdom, both in the literal world and over the spiritual forces, will be the KING of KINGS, the Lord Jesus Christ, the Jewish Messiah.*

4. It is important to realize that as knowledge of the kingdom is limited or withheld, we lose the understanding of Israel's election: why the Jewish people will endure, and why she is the object of God's choosing. Many misconceptions abound. Often people believe that heaven is our ultimate and last destination. But in fact, Heaven is a rather brief stop in comparison to the Messianic era. This is because we are living closer than all previous generations to the coming Kingdom. The Messianic Kingdom, (the

Millennial Reign of our Lord,) will last for 1000-years on earth. Afterward, God will bring the New Heavens and the New Earth. Hence, our next longest destination is the kingdom on earth with our Messiah. It is this plan of God that was always purposed for the earth. One prophet, Habakkuk, speaks of a time when the whole earth will be filled with the knowledge of the Glory of God.[xix]

5. Another misconception is that the future kingdom will be purely ethereal. In reality, it will be governmental, material, and spiritual. This governmental aspect is what we pray for in the Lord's Prayer in Matthew 6:10, *"thy kingdom come."* When we pray this prayer, we are beseeching the Lord to hasten to the earth His righteous government. It will have a land to rule, as the entire earth will be under Messiah's government, and His law will finally go out from Jerusalem to the uttermost parts of the earth.[xx] We notice than two people types will be on the earth; the incorruptible and corruptible. During this time, cities will need to be righteously ruled, as corruptible people will still be on the earth.[xxi] Yes, those that have returned with their glorified bodies will be privileged to co-reign with Messiah. These saints with glorified bodies are both Gentile and Jewish believers that have previously been raptured, and as noted, returned with *Yeshua* to co-reign with Him.[xxii] Included are those that were resurrected after *Yeshua*.[xxiii]

KINGDOM STUDY OUTLINE II

1. **THE MESSIANIC KINGDOM AND ORDER**: The Messianic Kingdom, is a designated order that comprises a Jewish branch of government as well as a Gentile branch. Organizationally, the absolute monarchy of the future kingdom will extend out from King Messiah, as authority will be delegated to other branches.

   - One is the resurrected king David. He will be a prince. Consider this extraordinary description of the David's future role, *"Afterward, the Israelites will return and seek the LORD their God and David, their king. They will come trembling to the LORD and his blessings on the last day" (Hosea. 3:5).*

   - The twelve Apostles will return to rule the twelve tribes of Israel. It is important to stress that David will not be serving as King and absolute monarch, but as noted, he will be one of many princes.

   *The Gentile nations will also have kings or rulers, but the they have their natural bodies while King David will have his resurrected body.

   1.a. The prophet Jeremiah reveals that the Jewish people will finally seek the one true God, and at the same time, have David their king: *"But they shall serve the LORD their God, and David their king, whom I will raise up unto them"* (Jeremiah 39:9, KJV). Other Jewish prophets envisioned a time when David returns: *"I will place over them one shepherd, my servant David, and he will tend them; he will tend them and be their shepherd. I the LORD will be their God and my servant David will be prince among them (Ezekiel. 34:23).* Accordingly, the chain of command will flow from *Yeshua* to Israel, and to the Gentile nations. This was His plan from the beginning. [xxiv]

2. THE GROANING FOR THE KINGDOM: The kingdom that all creation has been groaning for has been a global dream for every nation and tongue down through the millennia. [xxv] "The" Son has also been waiting to fulfill His final office as King over the earth. This will not be some quiet event. Like a crowd cheering on their runner that is about to cross the finish line, we will praise and worship our Lord as Israel comes to faith. The whole world will share in the glory of this grand finale, which the enemy has sought to destroy through the ages.

a. Finally, for some Gentiles who might feel excluded due to so much attention upon Israel, there will be a gentile branch of government (Revelation 20:4-6) parallel to a Jewish branch. Gentile believers who were raptured before the Great Tribulation, and those that were martyred, will rule with Messiah, alongside the Jewish saints during the Millennium.

b. The glorious and reigning martyrs that were persecuted and beheaded because they refused to worship the beast, or take his mark on their forehead, or persecute the Jewish people, will co-reign with the Messiah over the gentile nations. Consider these words of Isaiah, who gives a portrayal of the future temple ministry that awaits the Gentile:

> *"Also the sons of the stranger, that join themselves to the LORD, to serve him, and to love the name of the LORD, to be his servants, every one that keeps the Sabbath from polluting it, and takes hold of my covenant; Even them will I bring to my holy mountain, and make them joyful in my house of prayer: their burnt offerings and their sacrifices shall be accepted upon mine altar; for mine house shall be called a house of prayer for all people."*
>
> *(Isaiah 56:6-7)*

In conclusion, God gathers *"the outcasts of Israel, and will gather others to him,"* (Isaiah 56:1–8, KJV). The "Messianic era," or also known as the "Kingdom," "Millennial Reign," "Messianic Government," will tie everything together to form a complete picture of our Creator's intention when he breathed His first breath into a man. Israel, will, at last, find our resting place and purpose, and the Jew and the Gentile will cohabit the future order in peace and unity. Their distinction will be preserved as two siblings of the same family. One can see from this brief introduction to God's Sacred Mountain (the Messianic Kingdom), a mystery is solved that has lingered over mankind down through the ages; *the irrevocable call upon the Jewish people, and the purpose of God's choosing of Israel.*

- **PURPOSE OF THE KINGDOM: Jewish Election, Calling, and Future Purpose.** To prepare for any formal plan to reach the Jewish people, knowing these essential elements that have been in contention for much of the Christian era, reveals the historical wall that has been erected, and the challenges that Jewish outreach presents. Here we are introduced to the Messianic Kingdom, where and when we discover the "irrevocable" call, the purpose of Jewish Election. Generally speaking, the Messianic kingdom has been at the center of longing and prayer. But much confusion exists over this topic of the Millennial Kingdom even though it has been ordained from the eternities of time. Always envisioned, was Israel restored to her former glory, and Israel living in her fullness under the leadership of their Messiah. This fact is true today, as well.

1. The longing for the kingdom permeates the Christian Church also, but with a more ethereal concept. While her focus is on such images and realities as the cross, the resurrection, the ascension, and heaven, the Jew sees Jerusalem and Mt. Zion restored—The Christian sees the "New Jerusalem" coming down out of heaven, as described in Revelation 21:2.

2. However, the kingdom of God has permeated Christian teaching, while the kingdom of heaven has permeated Judaism. The words, "the kingdom of heaven," refer to the origin of this Kingdom. It speaks of the place from which the Kingdom is coming, and it is not the destination that we are going to; the Kingdom of Heaven is a kingdom of heaven, not a kingdom in heaven. Daniel makes the statement that the "God of heaven will set up a kingdom that will never be destroyed."[xxvi]

3. Although the Kingdom of Heaven is heavenly and governmental in character, angels do not descend to the earth to rule over man. This is significant to end time understanding, since the kingdom of Heaven, or the Messianic kingdom, pulls all things back towards God's original design. God uses it to return the earth to what He designed, and man will finally discover his place in God's creation.

4. The kingdom then becomes a vital key to unlocking end-time mysteries that have long captured the imaginations of God's people. Its characteristics are as follows: joy (Isaiah 9-3-4), glory (Isaiah 24:23), justice (Isaiah 9:7), full knowledge (Isaiah 11:1-2), instruction and learning (Isaiah 2:2-3), longevity of age (Isaiah 65:20) and harmony in the animal kingdom (Isaiah 11: 6-9; 65:25). Notice this area of full knowledge [xxvii]. In the future, the nations will finally discover God's plan regarding Israel and the Jewish people, which brings forward nothing less than what has been a source of contention: Jewish election in the future age. Let's explore further than this future time.

THE FUTURE AGE: YESHUA'S FINAL OFFICE: Mainly, the future Kingdom is a restorative age, and what we have already established: knowledge and understanding will fully be present for the first time since the Garden era. What is often overlooked is the final office of a threefold function that *Yeshua* will complete during this time. First, He came as a Prophet and pointed to Himself as the one that fulfilled over 300 prophecies, even that He would be rejected by His own. His second role is one that He is currently serving in as our High Priest. Today, He is sitting at the right hand of the Father making intercession for us. In the future Messianic kingdom, He will exercise His office as King. Then, following one thousand years, He will hand over the earth to His Father. [xxviii]

> **Daniel's Vision of a Mountain:** As noted earlier, Daniel saw this kingdom as a mountain that engulfed the entire earth. Images of mountains have long captured the imaginations of man. People revere them because they embody powerful forces beyond our control. For instance, a rising peak of a mountain captured in one's eye can be powerful. When you reach the summit of a mountain, you arrive at the highest level or degree that you can attain. Only then can one perceive every nuance of the landscape below it. One can see, for example, how a river is placed in relationship to the land that buffers it.
>
> Scripturally, mountains often represent kingdoms and places of spiritual power.[xxix] Nothing is more representative of this than the Messianic Kingdom or God's Sacred Mountain. When you reach this summit, you discover the important understanding of the Messianic Kingdom, and what God intends in the future. One captures how Israel and the Jewish people are positioned in relationship to the nations, along with Israel's God-given purpose. Essentially, what has been a mystery throughout Christian history is solved. There we discover why Israel has endured; why is she called the "Apple of God's Eye;[xxx]" and why she is called "the chosen people." [xxxi]

✡ **THE KINGDOM OF GOD / KINGDOM OF HEAVEN:** For a greater perspective on the future order, we must draw a distinction between the kingdom of God and the kingdom of Heaven. The Kingdom of God is universal, spiritual, angelic, limitless, and timeless. Nothing exists outside of it, and no one can escape it. Even the very cosmos and beyond is under it. For this reason, the kingdom of heaven (the Messianic age,) is inseparable from the kingdom of God.

The Psalmist in chapter 39 expresses a similar sentiment; *"Such knowledge is too wonderful for me, too lofty for me to attain. Where can I go from your Spirit? Where can I flee from your presence? If I go up to the heavens, you are there; if I make my bed in the depths, you are there."* Although the kingdom of God is limitless, the kingdom of heaven will rest upon the earth for a limited period of 1,000 years, and only after this does the kingdom of heaven become the kingdom God within each other. [xxxii] Since the kingdom of heaven or the Messianic age is governmental, we must discover what comprises this government, and what moves us closer to the purpose of Israel's election. This brings us to the purpose of the kingdom of Heaven.

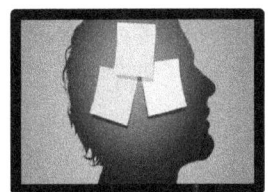

CRUCIFIED WITH THIEVES: Isaiah 53:12 *"Therefore I will divide Him a portion with the great, And He shall divide the spoil with the strong, Because He poured out His soul unto death, And He was numbered with the transgressors, And He bore the sin of many, and made intercession for the transgressors."* Matthew 27:36-38

GARMENT PARTED / LOT CAST: Psalm 22:17-19 *"I can count all my bones. They look, they stare at me; They divide my garments among them, And for my clothing they cast lots. But You, O LORD, be not far off; O You my help, hasten to my assistance."* Anguish? John 19:23-24

NOT A BONE BROKEN: Psalms 34:20 *"Many are the afflictions of the righteous, But the LORD delivers him out of them all. He keeps all his bones, Not one of them is broken."* John 19:31-33, 36

1. How does the Messianic Kingdom reveal God's purpose for Israel and the Jewish people?

2. Describe the relationship between the Messianic Kingdom and the Irrevocable call of the Jewish people in Romans 11:29.

3. Describe *Yeshua's* threefold office. Which final office remains to be fulfilled?

4. What two end time events must take place before the Second Coming of the Lord?

5. What does the Messianic Kingdom say about God's original design for this world?

SECTION IX

WHOSE LAND IS IT ANYWAY?

ISRAEL'S VISIONARY

WHOSE LAND IS IT ANYWAY

I

A historical struggle over the Promised Land as God covenanted with Abraham, then Isaiah, and Jacob, and then the generations that followed, has existed as a Geopolitical stone of stumbling. But any serious Bible student cannot escape that which God has woven throughout its pages as a provocative testimony of a people that have been set aside in a specific land—No other nation can make such claims. Do you know why?

> *"If statistics are right, the Jews constitute but one percent of the human race. It suggests a nebulous dim puff of stardust lost in the blaze of the Milky way. Properly, the Jew ought hardly to be heard of, but he is heard of, has always been heard of. He is as prominent on the planet as any other people, and his commercial importance is extravagantly out of proportion to the smallness of contributions to the world's list of great names in literature, science, art, music, finance, medicine, and abstruse learning are also away out of proportion to the weakness of his numbers. He has made a marvelous fight in this world, in all the ages; and had done it with his hands tied behind him. He could be vain of himself and be excused for it."*

- Mark Twain

Before we answer the question, "Whose Land Is It Anyway," we must provide a historical foundation of Israel's journey to the land in the context of the political environment and the challenges posed in the years preceding 1948. This topic is extensive, and volumes of works have been published on this very subject. But for our purposes, a brief overview and some important touchstones that formed Israel's path back to her land is provided. Ultimately, we answer the question: ***"Whose Land Is It Anyway?"***

Let us first note: numerous names are given in the Bible for Israel. There is the Land of the Hebrews (Genesis. 40:15), the Holy Land (Zechariah 2:12), the land of Jehovah (Hosea 9:3, Psalms. 85:1), the Land of Promise (Hebrews 11:9). For Bible students and teachers of prophecy, the birth of Israel in 1948 was one the greatest predictive events of our modern time. Take for example the combined passages of Leviticus. 26 and Ezekiel 4:3-6, to produce a prophetic prediction of Israel becoming a nation in 1948, 2,484 years before it happened to the day (See Appendices.) Also, remarkable. Abraham was born in 1948 BCE (Rashi's calculation of 1,948 years after creation). There is no nation on earth that is so spiritually and Biblically bound to their land as the Jewish people of Israel. Rabbi Hayim Halevy Donin says, "It is a land possessed by not only right of conquest and settlement but also a fulfillment of history, faith, and law."

> **ISRAEL'S VISIONARY**
> *"Four years ago, in speaking of a Jewish nation, one ran the risk of being regarded ridiculous. Today he makes himself ridiculous who denies the existence of a Jewish nation." (Theodor Herzl)*

The brainchild of the state of Israel was Theodor Herzl. A son of a wealthy banking family, Herzl was born in Hungry and moved to Vienna to work as a journalist. He never imagined that this move would spontaneously spark a prophetic fulfillment for the Jewish return to Zion.

Herzl was on assignment covering the infamous trial of a French captain, Alfred Dreyfus, who happened to be Jewish. Though the charges of passing French military secrets to Germany later proved to be false, Herzl witnessed anti-Jewish rallies, public outcries, and anti-Semitic slurs like, "A bas les Juifs" (Down with the Jews) and "A la mort les Juifs," (Death to the Jews). These early encounters with anti-Jewish hatred bore a realization in Herzl that if the Gentiles were given a chance, they would kill the Jew. He termed this the "Jewish problem." This event, coupled with other experiences and observations, convinced Herzl that anti-Semitism could not be defeated or cured, at best, it could only be avoided. He realized a Jewish state had to be established.

To begin, Herzl published a book in 1896 outlining this idea and titled the project, Der Judenstat (The Jewish State). The next year under his leadership, the First Zionist Congress convened in Basel, Switzerland. However, even as early as 1894 few were willing to lend support to the idea.

[OPPOSITIONISTS & ASSIMILATIONISTS]

As Herzl worked tirelessly in those early years for a Jewish State, he found that most people were in two categories: **Oppositionists,** and those that he termed **Assimilationists.** These were people who thought it would be better for Jewish people to assimilate into the nations. Their concern was more for the loss of Jewish wealth than the safety of the Jewish people.

With the rise of Nazi Germany, and the attempted extermination of all of European Jewry by Adolph Hitler, Herzl's worst fears, thirty some years following his death, were realized. On November 29, 1947, a coalition of nations finally agreed that the Jews needed a haven to call their own. Finally, the United Nations voted in support of a Jewish homeland. However, consistently linked to it was the idea to partition the Holy Land into two independent states. This was to bring about the internationalization of Jerusalem. But throughout this process, Arab opposition was well known; if Israel were granted her land, the Arab nations would ignite a war.

[DAYS OF WAR BEGIN]

Finally, on May 14, 1948, Israel declared her independence. Immediately, the allied forces of Syria, Lebanon, Jordan, Egypt, and Iraq defied the U.N. agreement and attacked Israel the following day. But Israel was ill equipped due to an international arms embargo. Then God raised up Czechoslovakia, who chose to sell her arms and supplies, which turned the tide of the war in Israel's favor.

Israel has endured three major wars since the 1948 War of Independence. There was the Sinai Campaign in 1956 between Israel and Egypt, the Six-Day War in 1967 with Nasser of Egypt, Jordan, and Syria, and the Yom Kippur War in 1973 when Egyptian and Syrian forces attacked Israel on two fronts. One can say unequivocally, war defines Jewish history. We can look back to ancient times to the capture of the Jerusalem temple in 165 BCE, or the invading Roman legions in 63 BCE, and the Jewish revolt in 66 and 67 AD. Rome's last conquest of

Jerusalem in 70AD sent 1 million Jews to their deaths; 97,000 Jews were captured, thousands more were sold as slaves throughout the cities of the Roman Empire, and untold thousands perished from starvation. The ancient Jewish historian Josephus writes in the "The War of the Jews," of the awful time of Jerusalem's destruction in 70 AD.

Conveyed with heart-wrenching detail is the Jewish connection to the Temple: "…hundreds of thousands lay dead in the streets of Jerusalem with their eyes fixed upon the temple." So relieved was Rome that the Jewish problem was solved that commemorative coins were minted that said Judea Capta. Historically, Israel is a nation that all countries struggle over. Therefore, the Jewish people have remained in a struggle for survival down through history.

[THE PROMISED LAND]

We turn our attention now to the Covenant, where we read about what God intended when He covenanted with Abraham. The covenant is found in Genesis 17:7-8: *"I will give as an everlasting possession to you and your descendants after you, and I will be their God."* But how did the land move from one to the other? Covenantal provisions never came through agreements or good will, or between man and man. Always, it came between God and man. Predictably, it often involved a clash with other people.

In 1948 when the Jewish people returned to their land, Israel had to settle the whole business by force. Even during ancient times in the land of Canaan, war was required to advance God's will. If you recall, Abraham and his clan moved between two powerful heathenish cultures, Babylonia and Egypt. In later years, the patriarch Abraham was brought into the War of the Kings (Genesis 14). It was a conflict that was comprised of an alliance of five kings that what would ultimately sweep his nephew, Lot, and his household away. However, Abraham walked as a conqueror throughout because God gave him a promise of an everlasting possession for him and all his generations. Similar circumstances befell Joshua when he had to take hold of the promise.

[ISRAEL TODAY]

Today, Israel is approximately 11,000 square miles, a mere fraction of its original 60,000 square miles when it was ruled over by David, and later his son Solomon. In 1947, a year before Israel's Independence, Arab states totaled 8,500,000 square miles. Compare this to what was considered Israel's administered areas of only 28, 500 square miles at the time of Jewish return to the Promised Land.

As one can see, the land has become smaller throughout the war years that followed. In 1978, the quantitative difference between Israel and her Arab neighbors in the territory, population, wealth, and arms, was overwhelming. The population of the Arab States was approximately 134,000,000 to Israel's small 3,500,000 people. The GNP (Gross National Product) of the Arab states, not factoring in inflation and increased oil production in 1967, was approximate $150 billion to Israel's tiny $13 billion. Given such disparities, Israel has struggled for her tiny sliver of the Promised Land. So why is a small state both in area and population despised by so many? The answer lies not in the Geopolitical sphere of course, but within the Spiritual.

[BORN TO STRUGGLE]

Thousands of years have transpired, and the Jew has repeatedly found herself against insurmountable odds. She is always facing enemies seeking to take more of her land and, regularly, labeling her as the scapegoat for tensions and terrorism. From one Presidential administration to the other, dividing Israel appears to be an imaginary panacea and cure-all for the Middle East's turbulent woes. It appears that Israel is a nation born to suffer.

Even in 1948, the Arab aversion to Israel has changed little from our modern day. Taken from a "Life Magazine" article back in June of 1967, the Arab-Israeli struggle is highlighted at the time; "For Arabs, Israel is an illegal fiction created out of former Arab lands by an imperialistic West, an alien culture that poses a continual threat to a visionary brotherhood of the Arab nations that surround it."

Given all that has been stated, nothing captures such political dialogue and fuels world tensions as Israel. Repeatedly, attempts have been made to excise the Jew from the Land through war and anti-Semitism, or the land itself from the Jew. Through political pressures to divide the land for the sake of peace in the Middle East, Israel is caught between two tensions: *"That which God has established, and that which the world seeks to alter."* At the center of such a historical turmoil resides a people who can trace their history and occupation to a homeland that is three thousand years old. In one word, if another nation invaded Israel, and if it were possible to displace every Jew from the land, Israel would cease to be as God created her. The reason was: *The land is tethered to the Jew as the Jew is tethered to the land—They are in fact self-defining of each other!* No other people group then possesses such a unique history and no other land is accompanied with specific promises that foretell of an extraordinary prophetic future. Israel rarely has time to ponder the conflicts of the past before new ones begin.

1. Why has Israel struggled for survival? Provide three Scripture references to support your answer.

2. Where can modern day "oppositionists" and "assimilationists" be found in Christian circles today?

WHOSE LAND IS IT?
II

To begin to draw close to answering the question; **"Whose Land Is It Anyway?"**, the answer may seem obvious, at least on the surface! But Biblically, God gave the land of Israel to Abraham (Genesis. 17:8) and his descendants through Isaiah, (Genesis. 26:2-5) then Jacob, whose name was changed to Israel, and his descendants who became the 12 tribes of Israel (Genesis. 28:1-4,13-14).

While all other nations own their land, no one owns Israel. Yes! No one owns Israel. God owns Israel and no other! What I mean to say is, Israel was given to the Jewish people through the Covenant. There from that instrument they became the Chosen stewards of the Promised Land. Always then, it will remain the land where the Jewish people are called to dwell. Thirteenth-century Exegete and biblical scholar, Moses Nachmanides, who interprets the phrase, **"*For the land is mine*,"** in Leviticus 25:23, notes that God is speaking to Israel through Moses with these words; *"You are but strangers, residents with me."*

Two other translations convey the same idea, *"The land must not be sold permanently because the land is mine and you are but aliens, and my tenants."* (TNIV) *"And remember, the land is mine, so you may not sell it permanently. You are merely my tenants and sharecroppers"* (NLT). In other words, the Jewish people were given the land of Israel for them to live in, but they do not own the land.

Consider that in the future kingdom, the millennium, Israel will be the center of power and government where the Messiah will establish His throne in Jerusalem. For this alone, no one can own the Holy Land other than God. He, in fact, holds what is known as the ***inalienable rights***, or what is considered the deed. The Jewish people, on the other hand, hold the **unalienable rights,** or, the **tenant contract.** Again, God holds the *inalienable* rights, while Israel holds the *unalienable* rights. This is explained further in the following.

[UNALIENABLE / INALIENABLE]

The differences between *unalienable* and *inalienable* is important. According to its earliest definition some 300 years ago, one can see the outline-meaning of Jewish claim to the land. It is also where we receive a hint of their continual right to occupy the land.

When it comes to this historical term, *unalienable,* most recognize it from the Declaration of Independence. But it is more ancient than that. Recall these words, *"We hold these truths to be self-evident, that all men are created equal, that they are endowed by their Creator with certain unalienable Rights."* The understanding of this word meant that an individual who possessed *unalienable* rights could only receive those rights from an authority greater than any human agency. The early framers of the Declaration of Independence recognized that only God could give man his rights. Also, in this word, *unalienable,* there is the word lien. A [lien] is a legal claim or a charge upon real or personal property for the satisfaction of some debt or duty.

For instance, one must first satisfy one's debt or service as it was in Bible times to gain personal property. This principle was seen between Laban and Jacob. Since *Unalienable* holds no lien, or, no authority, one cannot give, transfer, or sell those rights. If we were to apply this to land ownership, land could only be inherited from one generation to the next. It cannot be given away, sold, or granted to another. This is like the land of Israel. The Promised Land always moves from one Jewish generation to another, and it cannot be granted to another nation. However, because of the unalienable rights that the Jewish people have, they have no legal right to sell the land. Therefore, the Jewish people remain the chosen stewards of the land.

[INALIENABLE]

Let us now explore the meaning of the term, *inalienable*, where we once again notice the word lien again. But in this case, it contains the prefix "in," which signifies that power is vested in it. In other words, the lien is active, while in the word unalienable the lien is inactive. If one were to research this further and look up the word unalienable, you would be directed back to the word *inalienable,* because in our modern time the meaning is exactly the same. But three hundred years ago, these two words meant the exact opposite. This is brought to light when Thomas Jefferson's found himself at odds with the Declaration committee when he submitted his first draft of the *Declaration Independence.* Let's see why!

[THE DECLARATION COMMITTEE]

When the first draft of the Declaration of Independence was submitted to the Declaration Committee, they perceived great danger over Jefferson's choice of the word inalienable. Recalling what has been stated: inalienable meant that the one had the power to surrender or bargain their rights away. The Declaration Committee wondered how someone could take away or give away what God our Creator gave. Thankfully, the wording was changed to unalienable, which guarded our freedoms forever.

[ISRAEL'S UNALIENABLE RIGHTS]

All that has been stated reveals that the Jewish people possess the unalienable rights to the land that God promised them. But no other nation on earth has claimed to any portion of Israel. When the United States and other nations pressure Israel to divide the land, they violate God's *inalienable* rights, and Israel's *unalienable* rights as "the chosen stewards." This is a volatile mix for nations. Recall the fact that no nation other than Israel was told that their land would be the place that *Yeshua* would return to; only the Jewish people can trace their birth, history, and future, to their occupation of the Promised Land (Genesis 15:18-21, 28:13, Exodus 23:31).

[ISRAEL'S TENANT CONTRACT]

For deeper understanding we touch upon the covenant. The land agreement or covenant is God's permanent "tenant contract" with the Jewish people, and it will always remain this way! But the idea of a tenant contract in this context does not diminish the power of God's agreement with the Jew, because as mentioned, it is permanent, changeless, and irrevocable. It can be compared to someone providing you with a home to live in for you and your children, and your children's children, and extending to all their generations with one caveat—you do not own it, you cannot sell it, and you cannot give it to another, you must only take care of it.

From this understanding, the Jewish people are a bonded community by a divine contract, which is not abstract or concocted as their enemies often times assert. For this reason, nations that seek to place conditions and attachments to the Land that God transferred to [His] first born will never turn out well. To the weakening of our country, and in the ignorance of our administration, the U.S. has undertaken many actions to divide Israel for a Palestinian state. As noted earlier, this violates both Israel's unalienable rights as the tenant and God's inalienable rights as the Landowner. Let me illustrate it this way in a parable:

A landowner was going on a long journey. He gave charge of his vineyard and his home to his servants for them to occupy, care and protect it. Since the landowner had the inalienable rights, he had the power and authority to confer upon them this exclusive right to be his tenants. In turn, the servant received the unalienable rights. However, it did not take very long for hostility to arise between the legal tenant, and those wanting a portion of the landowner's vineyard. They did not realize that wanting claim to the land violated both the landowner's inalienable rights and the chosen servant's unalienable rights. The only one that could settle this long and enduring struggle was the landowner, The Lord Himself, upon his return.

NOTES:

1. What does it mean that God owns the land of Israel, yet, the land was given to the Jewish people? Provide three Scriptures to support your answer.

2. Explain the differences between "inalienable" and "unalienable". How does it apply to Jewish possession of the land of Israel, as well as God's relationship to the land?

CONCLUSION

Whose Land Is It Anyway? Simply, Israel belongs to the Jewish people. They alone are the chosen stewards, and they will forever be its tenants. As God owns the land, the world has always struggled over formulating a definition of Israel's right to the Promised Land. But the land of Israel was given to the Jewish people not as a reward, nor as a free-will gift. It was also not independent of Israel's choices. The blessings were dependent upon her obedience to Adonai.

To repeat what has been stated: The Jewish people are the "chosen stewards." A steward is a person who manages another's property or one who administers the affairs as the agent of another. In Israel's case, the Jew is the chosen agent and elected people that God chose to administer and manage the estate of God, Israel.

As an emerging Jewish-centric body is getting a heart for Zion, a deep understanding of God's heart for Israel and the Jewish people is found today. A Heart for Zion can be defined as a genuine love for Israel as a covenant land and people, coupled with a sense of duty to assist financially and prayerfully the Jewish calling. This not only pertains to the land of Israel but the Jewish calling throughout the Diaspora. In a word, it is a heart truly bent towards the Jew whether in Israel, the United States, or the nations.

1. **The Jewish people are the chosen stewards,** *"for the land is mine"* **Leviticus 25:23. Note that God is speaking to Israel through Moses with these words,** *"you are but strangers, residents with me."*

2. **Israel holds the unalienable rights—God holds the inalienable rights.**

SECTION X

✡ **WHY ISRAEL WILL ENDURE FOREVER**

✡ **THE TWELVE DISTINCTIONS OF ISRAEL**

WHY ISRAEL WILL ENDURE FOREVER
"TWELVE DISTINCTIONS OF ISRAEL"

Do you know why Israel will endure forever while most nations will disappear? Here we provide the answer, and another reason that Jewish ministry hold a tremendous prophetic element not seen in any other people group. In this section we introduce the reader to 12 distinctions of Israel. Solidly rooted in God's Word, they are not subjective. But they are 12 foundations stones to understanding the Irrevocable Call of the Jewish people.

In the Old Testament, we learn of Israel's genesis, her wanderings, and her individual and often intimate relationship with God. In the New Testament, we witness her final victory that takes place simultaneously with the culmination of the age, and the genesis of the Kingdom upon Messiah's return; this is called the Messianic Kingdom. But let us agree to the fact that no other nation holds such a clear and distinct role in the future as Israel, which endures from the first chapter of the Bible to the last. In fact, Israel is the only nation with such a well-defined prophetic future in the Scriptures.

Though many other nations have risen and fallen, (something that the United States is not immune to) Israel will endure to the end of days. At the same time, no other geography has been fought over for no financial gain other than Israel. Up until recent history, Israel has had no natural gas or potential oil. More, half of its land mass is a desert.

When it comes to the idea of distinction, Biblically speaking, many cite that the Jew is not dissimilar from the Gentile, nor Israel from the nations. This is often based on the New Covenant doctrine that states there is no difference between the Jew or Gentile, Israel, and the nations, as seen in Galatians 3:28 and Colossians 3:11. But excluding such principles as salvation, grace, and sanctification, a great difference does exist between Jew and Gentile, Israel and the nations. In fact, to apply such a standard of universality to Israel and the Jewish people ignores the comprehensive mention of the Jew and Israel throughout the Word of God. No honest Bible student can deny their distinctiveness.

From Genesis to Revelation Israel is referred to in Scripture well over 2000 times. This is the "law of repetition," which alone brings forth uniqueness. It is the same principle by which God repeats some truth, or subject, that is already given, but provides details not given before; this is also known as the "law of recurrence". It does not cease here; Israel is a tipping point upon which other events depend.

In 1948, the world's attention was captured when the Jewish people miraculously returned to the land of Israel following their dispersion in 70 AD. Although immediately following her independence in 1948 were wars and struggles, Israel's rebirth remains one of "the" essential indexical events of our modern time, and a pre-condition to other prophetic fulfillments. But consider the extraordinary future that awaits Israel and her overall distinctiveness, before we break down the twelve distinctions of Israel.

Can another nation claim this unusual condition for their existence? No! To uproot Israel then, as some have presumed, would dislodge the cog that holds the wheel on its axle. To be sure, prophecy cannot roll forward without her. In sum, Israel holds perpetuity and exclusivity. Causatively, she remains the source of world tensions, as well as a blessing. No other geography is the source of worldwide tensions as the Temple Mount; it remains "the" hotbed of political dialogue; a fireball causative of war and violence; and a stumbling block for nations.

With all of this distinctiveness, rarely is Israel celebrated. Israel is tolerated at best. And unquestionably, few nations are aware of how their destinies are intertwined with Israel. Let's break down these points further to discover the broad elements of Israel's distinctiveness, and why Israel will endure forever!

KEY POINT Israel will become the world's threshing floor when every nation and tongue comes to worship the King of Kings (Zechariah. 14:16).

Israel will be the place where the future seat of power is located when the Lion of Judah establishes His throne in Jerusalem (Isaiah. 9:6-7, 66:1 Psalms 122).

Israel will be the center of worldwide convocations as the nation's come to Jerusalem for the Millennial feasts (See the last chapter of Zechariah).

Israel will no longer be disfavored by the nations, but worldwide favor will be bestowed upon her. (Deuteronomy 15:6, 28:12, Zechariah 8:23).

Israel will be the place where God finally purifies the nations of the north (Russia) as she is destroyed upon Israel's mountains (Ezekiel. 38, 39).

Israel is the only nation that possesses the blessing and cursing doctrine. No other nation or people remain the cause and effect of blessings or cursing, other than the Jewish people. Genesis 12:3 states, *"those that bless the Jew will be blessed, and those that curse the Jew will be cursed."*

NOTES:

THE TWELVE DISTINCTIONS OF ISRAEL

1. THE LAW OF SEPARATION & ELECTION

In this first distinction, we discover the law of Election, which explains Israel's survival better than any human reasoning can offer. Fundamentally, it is based upon the fact that everything has a particular purpose, coupled with a divine plan to bring forth the will of our Creator. This can apply to one individually, corporately, as with the nation of Israel. Essentially, nothing is created randomly or out of chaos. This also speaks to the Law of *Separation*, and parallel to it, the law of *Distinction*. "

Purpose" links the principles of *Election*, *Distinction*, and *Separation* together. What I mean to say is that one is the result of the other. Yet principles of separation and distinction are seen throughout creation itself. There is a distinction between day and night. The seventh day of the week, *Sabbath,* is distinct from all other days. Money has a distinction as the tithe is separated from all other money. Nations and geographies all possess God-given distinctions. This principle also defines the family of God—we are to be a people separated from all other people (1 Peter. 2:9).

With this principle in mind, consider the fact that Israel was forged for separation. This not only guaranteed that she would be a distinct people and a unique nation, it assured that she would be a point of contention in the world; *separation and distinction always breed contention and competition.* Here is her unique calling from Deuteronomy. 7:6, *"For you are a people holy to the Lord your God. The Lord, your God, has chosen you out of all the peoples on the face of the earth; you are to be his people, his treasured possession."*[xxxiii]

As we look further, God selected Israel not because of their strength, size, or might.[xxxiv] In fact, they were the smallest and the weakest of people groups. Still, Israel was chosen, (also called the elected of God). This makes Israel formidable. Longer than anyone can remember, there has been this nation, Israel, resting over the body of Christ, and the world. Her calling and future purpose are called the *irrevocable calling* in Romans 11:29. God's choosing of Israel is simply and profoundly based upon divine "calling" and "election" as we have discussed.^{xxxv}

> ***For this reason, alone, Israel has remained in the pupil of God's eye, and forever He will watch over them! However, should we stop at this principle of separation and election, we would miss a full picture of God's choosing of Israel and the Jewish people's final place in the world!***

2. ISRAEL'S SUPERNATURAL BIRTH

The second distinction that we can see between Israel and all other nations is the manner of her birth. In 1948 following two thousand years of wandering, Israel was born. Interestingly, Abraham was born in 1948 BC. Of course, Israel came into being thousands of years before their independence in 1948 by way of the Abrahamic Covenant. Its details are found in Genesis 15-17. As noted, Israel was born through the Abrahamic Covenant when God first came to Abram, who later became Abraham. God then advanced the nation from Abraham to Isaiah, then to his son Jacob, and to his twelve sons, which became known as the twelve tribes of Israel.

However, no other nation was born out of such unusual circumstances. Other nations came out of human conquest, imperialism, power, land expansion, or seeking religious freedom as the United States. Not so with Israel. She was born out of the crucible of divine intent the moment God came to a man, Abraham, and began to form a nation. When God covenanted with Abraham, already Abraham had a son, Ishmael, born thirteen years earlier. Abraham's reaction is often overlooked, *"If only Ishmael would live before You!"* (Genesis 17:18).

- ✡ Abraham seems to imply that he wanted Ishmael to perpetuate his special relationship with God. But God states, *"my covenant I shall establish with Isaiah."* God affirms to Abraham that only Isaiah, the son you will have with Sarah, can be your true heir. Immediately between Ishmael and Isaiah, we see the principles of distinction, separation, and election once again.

- ✡ We also discover the strife that follows when one is called over the other. Consider the following: Ishmael came into the world by natural means, while Isaiah came through a supernatural event. Sarah, if you recall, was well beyond childbearing years (Genesis 18:11; Hebrews 11:11). Ishmael was circumcised at the age of thirteen, (Genesis 17:25) the age of daat (awareness). Isaiah, on the other hand, was circumcised as an eight-day-old infant when a person is not even aware of what is taking place, much less of its significance. (Genesis 21:4).

- ✡ Ishmael represents a natural relationship, one based on a person's nature and understanding. The relationship of Isaiah to Abraham and God's purpose then is based solely upon a supernatural bond.

- ✡ It follows that Israel was to become a distinct nation marked by the supernatural. Her history, well, was shaped only from the supernatural. Even her past wars from one to the next have been over something larger than politics, wealth, or geography. Few if any have been waged over the worship of the One True God, as with Israel. Consider this brief list of remembrances that were founded upon a demonic enemy seeking to rob from the people of God the worship of the One True God.

3. ISRAEL: A PRIESTLY NATION:

Distinction three brings forward the idea that God's purpose for Israel was to be a holy nation. Dennis Prager and Joseph Telushkin write in, *Why The Jews*, explaining so eloquently Jewish calling: *"Judaism's fundamental and important component of uniqueness asserts that the 'One True God' revealed Himself to the Jew. That He is the 'One' God of all the world. For all other nations, no other god is be worshiped. All others are false, and that this God makes moral demands upon every person and nation. Israel then was given a mission to propagate the principles of belief and the relationship of The One True God. This is something that no other nation can claim in their history."*

✡ No other nation was chosen to share their ***institutions, virtues, prayers, festivals, seventh day Sabbath rest, or first-fruit offerings.*** Take for example Succoth. Israel was required to bring as first fruits offering, 70 bullocks, on behalf of the nations. This was one of the earliest acts of intercession on the part of priestly Israel (Leviticus 23:34).

✡ Isaiah writes in chapter 42:6 *"I will keep you and will make you to be a covenant for the people and a light for the Gentiles"* (NIV). This passage reveals that Israel was given the mission to make people recognize the Almighty's sovereignty and to help them believe in Him; to bring to the world *Hashem's* rules, ethics, and instructions from Torah——The Jewish people still stand as of now a future people, who will fulfill this forthcoming role of a *Chosen People*.

We also learn that Israel was to be *"a kingdom of priests and a holy nation"* (Exodus 19:6). Through Israel, nations were to see that when Israel obeyed God they were blessed. When they disobeyed God they were punished (Deuteronomy 28). A special note needs to be made here: While many would wrongly maintain that Israel forfeited both this particular bond and calling upon their rejection of their Messiah, the bond between them and God is unbroken (Jeremiah 31:35-37), and their calling is irrevocable (Romans 11:29). In the future, all of God's original design as it pertains to Israel and the Jewish people, will be restored.

3A. ISRAEL AND THE NATIONS: When it comes to Israel's relationship to the nations, consider the following:

No other country besides Israel has been assigned to be a servant and priest to the nations through which the Messiah would come (Genesis 12:1-3, John 3:16).

God promised only to Israel that all nations would be blessed if they bless the Jew and cursed if they curse the Jew. (Isaiah 42:6, Genesis 12:3). What other nation and people holds such a key to blessing and cursing? The answer is none!

4. DIVINE PROVIDENCE

This fourth distinction recognizes how Israel came into being by divine providence. Out of all other nations, Israel alone was called forth by the One True God as noted in distinction two. He also brings forth divinely called people to advance His will as recorded in Hebrews 11. For instance, Abraham was chosen to begin Jewish history; Moses was selected to bring the Israelites out of Egyptian bondage, then to Sinai, and the borders of the Promised Land; Joshua was chosen to lead them finally into the Promised Land.

> **REVIEW:** Theodor Herzl (1860-1909), a non-biblical figure in history, was raised up by God to fulfill prophecy. Herzl is the founder of modern day Zionism which became the path of return for the Jewish people back to the Promised Land following two thousand years of wandering. What happened since Israel's inception, and what took place between Abraham and God, were many wars, difficulties, and tumult with the nations. But in the end, and according to prophecy, the resettlement of the Jewish people in 1948 was as much Jewish as it was God. This last statement may seem obvious, but it is good to recall the supernatural once again in God's dealings with Israel.
>
> ✡ First: It was Jewish because they are a particular people for God's purpose, and they are tethered to the land like no other. In the words of Rabbi Hayim Halevy Donin, "It is a land possessed by not only right of conquest and settlement but also a fulfillment of history, faith, and law."
>
> ✡ Second: Even though the Jewish people have struggled and contended for the land as Joshua did for the Promised Land, God orchestrated every

detail of their return as He did with Moses when he delivered the Israelites out of Egypt.

So regardless of their historical plight or their modern day struggles, their city Jerusalem is sure to shine again.[xxxvi] Jacob's tents will be restored, and the millennial palace of our Lord will sit in its proper place. One may quibble about the extent and pervasiveness of Jewish suffering and their supernatural survival, their ultimate and miraculous return to the Promised Land is something that no one can deny. The fact is, Israel will remain an energizing force of much prophetic significance.

5. THE JEW ENDURES

The Jewish people continue to demonstrate this rare ability to emerge from tyranny and social injustice. There is an unrelenting *chutzpa* (courage,) seen in them while facing their largest and strongest foes. In 2015, the leader of this tiny nation, Israel, stood proudly and confidently before the Congress of the United States reaffirming their conviction and commitment, to remain free, and undeterred to defend themselves. Few have the chutzpa of Prime Minister Benjamin Netanyahu of Israel. How Israel has withstood wars by Arab nations totaling millions of people, and nations whose land masses are in the millions, testifies to this principle of distinction. Israel confounds the experts, and continues to rise higher politically, financially, and militarily.

6. THE FUTURE KINGDOM

The sixth distinction takes us into the future. As the ancient Israelites went into captivity for their sins, they lost their national prominence and spent many years wondering in the desert. Eventually, the 12 tribes of Israel did settle in the land known as Israel. God chose the land of Israel for a bright and enduring future that is yet to unfold. This future calling has a specific purpose that is misunderstood because it remains postured in the future kingdom. Yet the contention over it—for it—and around it has endured throughout history. Only in the future kingdom to come, when God restores Israel to a position of leadership in the world,[xxxvii] will a humbled and obedient people Israel take their leadership role in the world that God intended for her. Here are more details of this time.

7. THE WIFE OF JEHOVAH

Passionate and enduring, filled with intimate language, the Bible presents Israel as the Wife of Jehovah. [xxxviii] A unique relationship to God is seen here that no other nation can claim. Although Israel is seen going through a relationship with God that moves from a "courtship" to a "marriage," then sadly into a "separation" and "divorce," she is gloriously restored to her Husband.[xxxix] The language that describes these stages is poignant at every stage. It is important to clarify, that the wife of Jehovah is distinct from the Bride of Christ in the New Testament. If this distinction is not preserved, the injury is done to the relationship between Israel and God, as well as to the Church. Although all Gentiles and Jews that accept *Yeshua* make up the Bride of Christ during this New Covenant age; Israel remains the wayward wife of Jehovah awaiting restoration to her Husband.

8. THE LAND IS MINE

While all other nations own their land, Israel is the only country and geography on earth that no one owns. Again, this is a distinction from all other nations on earth. To be exact, God owns Israel and no other! Israel was given to the Jewish people through the Covenant that God made with Abraham. His seed was to become the Chosen Stewards of the Promised Land until Messiah's return. But it will always remain the Promised Land where the Jewish people were called of God to dwell.

The famous thirteenth-century Exegete and biblical scholar, Moses Nachmanides, interprets the phrase, *"For the land is mine"* in Leviticus 25:23, Here God is speaking to Israel through Moses: *"You are but strangers residents with me."* Two other translations convey the same idea, *"The land must not be sold permanently because the land is mine and you are but aliens, and my tenants"* (TNIV). *"And remember, the land is mine, so you may not sell it permanently. You are merely my tenants and sharecroppers"* (NLT).

In conclusion, no one can own the Holy Land other than God, and He holds the inalienable rights or the deed. The Jewish people hold the unalienable rights or the tenant contract. Consequently, no other nation on earth has a claim to it. It should also be noted, Israel does not possess the right to sell off any portion of the land that God gave to them. So when the United States and other nations pressure Israel to divide the land, they violate God's inalienable rights, along with Israel's unalienable rights as "the chosen stewards." This is a volatile mix for nations that will never turn out well. Always it will bring cursing and prolonged difficulties.

Recall the fact, that God gave no other nation a specific land that He called His own. No other nation was told that their land would be the place that *Yeshua* would return to. Only the Jewish people can trace their birth, history, purpose, and future, to their occupation of the Promised Land (Genesis 15:18-21; 28:13; Exodus 23:31).

9. A DISTINCT IDENTITY

In the Scripture, the Jewish people are described in some ways that sets them apart from the nations. They are called, *"God's First Born Son"* (Exodus 4:22-23), the *"Apple Of His Eye"* (Proverbs 7:2, Zechariah 2:8, Psalm 17:8), *"His Chosen People"* (Deuteronomy 7:6-9), *"My Called"* (Isaiah 48:12), and *"A Peculiar Treasure"* (Exodus 19:5). *"Now, therefore, if ye will obey my voice indeed, and keep my covenant, then ye shall be a peculiar treasure unto me above all people: for all the earth is mine."* This area of distinction does not cease here. The following was noted in our introduction and is worthy of mention again. No other nation was given the covenant of circumcision, as a means to make a physical distinction between them, and the nations. (Genesis 17 Acts 7:8).

- ✡ No Other Nation other than Israel will be the international gathering place to worship the Lord (Zechariah 14:16; Isaiah 66 18; Revelation 7:9, 5:9).
- ✡ No other nation other than Israel will be the resting place where the Throne of Yeshua, the King of Kings, and, Lord of Lords, will reside (Jeremiah 3:17).

10. CARRIERS OF THE MESSIANIC SEED

The greatest of all distinctions remains God's choosing of the Jewish people to be the progenitor of the Messianic seed. God chose the nation of Israel over all other people on earth to be His special people, and the tribe of Judah to be the through which Jesus Christ the Jewish Messiah would be born.

God first promised the Messiah after Adam and Eve's fall into sin (Genesis chapter 3). Then God confirmed that the Messiah would come from the line of David.[xl] For this the Apostle Paul tells the Gentile Christian world that they should show their appreciation of this blessing that befell them, by sharing in their material blessings (Romans 15:27). In other words, because the majority of Jews rejected the Messiah, a debt of gratitude should be felt on the part of gentile believers, that they in turn would bless the Jewish people.

11. ISRAEL AND WORLDWIDE REVIVAL

In the book of Revelation, chapter 7, a large number of those who were sealed, 144,000 in fact, came from the twelve tribes of Israel. In verse 9 of the same chapter, an innumerable host is identified as coming out of the Great Tribulation; every nation and tongue are standing before the Throne. It has long been interpreted that these 144,000 are the latter day Jewish evangelists that bring about a great end time revival of souls; the fruit of their labor is the *"great multitude that no one can count."* Hence, the Jewish people bring about "The" end time revival before the Second Coming of Messiah.

12. KEY TO THE SECOND COMING

In Matthew 23: 37-39, some of the most passionate words of our Lord are spoken towards the very end of His ministry: *"Jerusalem, Jerusalem, you who kill the prophets and stone those sent to you, how often I have longed to gather your children together, as a hen gathers her chicks under her wings, and you were not willing."* He states a tragic consequence, *"For I tell you, you will not see me again until you say, "Blessed is he who comes in the name of the Lord."* It is only upon Israel's recognition of their Messiah, whom they have pierced that the return of the Lord will occur.[xli] Consequently, the Jewish people and Israel's salvation is a key to the Second Coming of Messiah!

 **WHO ENTERS THE KINGDOM?** A future judgment takes place in the Valley of Jehoshaphat that is spoken of in Matthew 25, and importantly, specific to the Jewish people. This passage is often misquoted and used to impart a heart for the poor and the needy. But this future event takes place upon *Yeshua's* return before entering the Kingdom of Heaven, or the Messianic age. Those according to the flesh and natural seed of Abraham are *Yeshua's* brethren, the Jewish people.

Throughout the book of Acts, Paul addresses his Jewish brothers 45 times. In most every instance he is speaking to a Jewish audience and His Jewish brethren. We should note, salvation is first and always in the belief in *Yeshua*. But the actions of this later group, the goat gentiles, is damning evidence of their allegiance to the anti-Christ.

Consequently, led by the anti-Christ and his armies, the goat gentiles join in the greatest persecution of the Jewish people ever in human history. Furthermore, due to their allegiance to the anti-Christ, the Goat Gentiles forfeit their entrance into the Messianic kingdom, while the sheep Gentiles enter into the Messianic Kingdom!

1. Why is the distinction between the Bride of Christ and the Wife of Jehovah important to maintain?

2. Who comprises the Wife of Jehovah and the Bride of Christ?

SECTION XI

APPLYING WHAT WE HAVE LEARNED

INDISPUTABLE FACTS OF THE MESSIAH

PRAYING WITH A JEWISH PERSON

APPLYING WHAT WE HAVE LEARNED

Congratulations, you have come to what is the most important part of this training manual; learning how to convey the gospel of the Jewish Messiah to the Jewish people. Though everyone will communicate through their own style, I have provided an example of myself as a Jewish person communicating to another Jewish person the gospel of Messiah. This will provide a unique window into how the Gospel can be communicated given the wealth of information and training that we have offered.

Mazal Tov! You have chosen to take a journey to learn about *Yeshua haMashiach*, that hundreds of thousands of Jewish people have discovered since He came. Your effort to consider this is likely filled with curiosity as well as courage, and some apprehension. But it takes Chutzpa to question things that might seem unquestionable. I assure you when one asks such questions as those prompted here, "THE" "Truth of all truths" comes into view, and life comes into a certain balance. In other words, life is about to get exciting!

Before we begin this journey an introduction to the many Jewish prophecies is essential. Let me put it this way: Often we read in advance about a certain place that we are planning to visit, so we when we arrive we understand its historical and cultural context. In a similar way, we are preparing for a journey, one more profound than any historical place that one could visit.

First, we speak of the long-held belief within Judaism in the concept of redemption. An entire book in our Torah is dedicated to it, Leviticus. The G-d of Abraham, Isaiah, and Jacob in fact, set the plan of salvation, or redemption of creation. It is no surprise then, this principle has been revealed throughout the Torah, (First Five Books,) the *Tanakh*, (the entire Old Testament,) and confirmed by the latter Jewish writers of the *Brit Chadasha*. However, Judaism and our traditional understanding maintain that these latter Jewish writings, cannot apply to Jewish dialogue on Jewish Messianic belief, or such principles as redemption. We set this aside for now as we will return to this later. Here one will challenge Jewish tradition because we are looking for truth, or, the emet. (truth)

Something that immediately comes into focus is that the whole Bible is a Jewish book. The authors of the Bible, both the former and latter, are joined by their common binding thread of Judaism. For instance, Matthew, or Levi was a Tax Collector; Paul was a Jewish scholar and a former Pharisee, all were observant Jews just as you would find today in Orthodox and Conservative communities. After all, how can we be Jewish without our beloved Torah and the recorded dealings of God with our people? We also have a long-standing and spiritual richness in Jewish life that is comprised of beautiful, meaningful traditions, wrapped around the Biblical Feasts and Holy days. All have endured for thousands of years. The latter writings of Rabbi Paul, together with an entire book dedicated to Jews and Judaism, (the book of Hebrews) encompasses 26 other books of Jewish import to consider.

While Judaism is the foundation upon which Christianity came forth, there is no need to depart from the Old Testament to find our Jewish Messiah of two thousand years ago. The subsequent Jewish writings, the New Testament, are replete with recorded fulfillments which correlate to hundreds of earlier prophecies that the Jewish people understood—longed for as well. In fact, these Scriptures are as Jewish as the former, the *Tanakh*. Together, they form a complete covenantal story that is Jewish in its entirety.

Woven throughout the Old Testament, we find prophecies of "The Coming One," the Jewish Messiah. He came to forewarn those whom He loved—the Jewish people—so that they would be aware and not miss the blessed opportunity. After all, two thousand years ago, the Jewish people knew that the Messiah would come and fulfill the writings of the prophets at that exact time in history. As the Jewish people received His message two thousand years ago, thousands of Jews throughout the past two millennia have entered this understanding, and thousands receive it today. Jewish Messianic hope looked to an individual that would give hope and bring Shalom—peace. He would give much more than one could ever have imagined. What would He give?

First, He would come to restore a right relationship with G-d, not only for the Jewish people but for all mankind. We can lose sight of the fact, that the Jewish people were always expected to impart to the goyim (gentiles), the principles of the One True God, and it was God's design that both groups would come to a knowledge of the Jewish Messiah.

Second, our Messiah would release us from the burdensome task of achieving right standing with G-d, through an unending sacrificial system that was difficult to maintain. To know, *Maschiach* then requires not the observance of *Mitzvot,* good deeds, sacrifices, or giving a portion of our income to Tzedakah. Although these are honorable for Jewish people, they are not required to come to know our Messiah or to achieve right standing before G-d. Through Maschiach then, one does not need to go to a Rabbi to learn the Torah and other Scriptures from our Tenakh. A child could even understand Messiah's words.

- One of the most important prophets, Jeremiah, stated this in chapter 31; *"This is the covenant I will make with the people of Israel after that time," declares the Lord. "I will put my Torah* תּוֹרָה *in their minds and write it on their hearts. I will be their God, and they will be my people. No longer will they teach their neighbor, or say to one another, 'Know the Lord, 'because they will all know me, from the least of them to the greatest."*

- Through Maschiach, G-d would plant within His people the heart, and spirit, and understanding of the Torah; His people would then find the true way, which is the true meaning of Torah תּוֹרָה.

- In the following, we discuss the most important Biblical Messianic prophecies that *Yeshua* fulfilled. We search for what Abraham Joshua Heschel addresses in his book, "Man Is Not Alone: A Philosophy of Religion." He writes about the "expectedness of meaning," and notes, "the certainty of whatever exists must be worthwhile, that whatever is real must be compatible with a thought, is at the root of all our thinking, feeling and volition. It is the reason's oracle of axiom on its vindications we stake all that we possess."

He further states, we search for some intrinsic quality in reality that would exhibit its significance, we are sure that the hidden and unknown will never turn out to be absurd or meaningless (*Man Is Not Alone: A Philosophy of Religion, Noonday Press*) Heschel's words defines our quest here. We search for that intrinsic quality that exhibits significance. When we find it, we'll; we discover an axiom we will stake all that we possess.

Something that may not be compatible with our thinking, but wholly compatible with our Scriptures, is the fact that *Yeshua* was human and yet divine. At this moment, you might see this as a point of departure. You may wish to stop reading or hearing what is being said. But wait a moment, though this concept is hard to receive as a Jew, let alone fit within our traditional Jewish understanding, let's shed another light upon it.

As we study Messiah's life as prophesied by the Jewish writings, it becomes plain that mankind could never have brought the endless stream of proofs and prophetic fulfillments that were completed by *Maschiach*, if in fact, He was not the prophesied one. On the contrary, the evidence discloses an individual who can be nothing less than supernatural, given the facts of his birth, life, and death. We find ourselves once again challenged to the core as Jews. But it will dawn upon us, that two thousand years ago, in the city of Jerusalem, thousands of Jewish people found that intrinsic quality that was noted earlier of great significance.

In the following, we discover that the things that we hold dear—the Torah, the writings of the Prophets, our Holy Days, and Sabbath days—never become obsolete when we come to an understanding of our *Maschiach*. Rather, they are constant, consistent, and over-arching from one era to another, and, from one generation to the next. On other words, Jewish belief in *Maschiach* is as Jewish as Matzo Ball soup and Gefilte fish. Here are some facts:

- ✡ When we as Jewish people accept the Jewish Messiah, never does it alter the fact that they remain Jewish. Messiah was Jewish! In every way, He was raised Jewish, lived Jewish, and his purpose in coming was first to His own Jewish people. Again, our adventure here challenges Jewish tradition (and even Christian tradition.)

✡ When it comes to our traditions, we know that they are vitally important to our culture, and they have kept our people together for thousands of years. They have woven us together people to such a degree that our traditions have defined us as Jews. But we must also keep in mind, tradition, though it is the transmission of important customs and beliefs, isn't always based on the facts, as we might assume. For this reason, we consider the following, particularly when it comes to the Jewish *Maschiach*.

MORE FACTS TO CONSIDER

YESHUA'S UNUSUAL BIRTH: When considering the Messiah, many Messiah types have come and gone. Yet none has transformed the world as *Yeshua*; none was spoken of with exact accuracy hundreds of years before His birth; none died and rose according to the exact predictions of the Jewish prophets, and none was born to such supernatural and unprecedented occurrences. Then, according to writings that are exclusively Jewish, Maschiach would be called, Messiah, Prophet, Priest, King, Lord, Judge, and Immanuel! One of our major prophets of Judaism, Yeshayahu, (Isaiah) prophesied that Maschiach would be conceived to a virgin. This is a pretty supernatural event alone! Here are his words; *"Therefore the Lord himself will give you a sign: The virgin will conceive and give birth to a son and will call him Immanuel."* (Isaiah 7:14; Matthew 1:18,25; Luke 1: 26-38).

The foregoing might again be hard to believe or comprehend. But isn't it true that all of Jewish history is difficult to comprehend in the natural mind? What I mean to say is: Only by faith and belief do we embrace our Torah completely and the supernatural deliverances of our people. The parting of the Red Sea, or the oil that lasted 8 days, and the favor that Esther received from a King that saved our people, are all supernatural. Consider the rebirth of our nation in 1948 following thousands of years of wandering. Jewish history is inherently supernatural through and through. And the fact that we have survived is a miracle in of itself!

So, at what point in our history do we stop believing in the miraculous and supernatural. A virgin birth is supernatural along with the comprehensive narrative of our people. Even upon His coming, a messenger of God (according to Malachi 3:1) was foretold centuries before he came. I am referring to John the Baptist who by no coincidence was a member of an Orthodox community called the Essenes, and also known as the Qumran community. We have in the Holy Scriptures hundreds of Messianic prophecies extending over hundreds of years. Their fulfillment is found only in one! One person, whose short thirty-year life span proved in every way that he was our Messiah, *Yeshua HaMaschiah*. In the last three years of Messiah's life, the most compelling promises and prophecies were fulfilled. Contrary to the Messiah, all other religious leaders have had to live out their entire lives to establish their religion; some were even established generations after. None were spoken of hundreds of years before they were born like *Yeshua*, and no one accomplished what He did.

Our Messiah was the only one that entered and left this world through such extraordinary and supernatural means, leaving behind an unending influence on the world in such a short period of time—an estimated 3 ½ years. Finally, no other than *Yeshua* became the subject of Old Testament prophecies that speak pointedly and exclusively of *Yeshua*. He alone accomplished the purposes of the Jewish writers, as they carefully pointed to the person, words, and works of *Maschiach*.

YESHUA'S TIME OF BIRTH:

One of the most extraordinary aspects of *Maschiach* was His time of birth. In no other time in history could He have been born. In 70AD when the temple was destroyed, all the genealogical records were destroyed as well. As a consequence, no determination would ever be possible henceforth to validate one's Messianic claims and its important lineage. Miraculously, this was predicted in the first book of the Torah, Genesis 49:10, which affirmed this; *"The scepter will not depart from Judah, nor the ruler's staff from between his feet, until he to whom it belongs shall come and the obedience of the nations shall be his."* Hence, the Messiah had to come before the scepter departed from Judah, and the Jewish people were scattered throughout the diaspora when they lost their national prominence and status.

YESHUA'S PLACE OF BIRTH

A third unusual aspect of Messiah was his place of birth; He must be born in the city of Bethlehem. Consider the fact that Yosef, or Joseph, the father of Yeshua, was not even from Bethlehem when Miriam, or Mary, conceived *Yeshua*. Neither had he any intention of going to Bethlehem at such an important time in her pregnancy.

- ✡ Yet, G-d foretold that *Maschiach* would be born in that very town. He foreknew the events that would bring that couple to that very city, as He foreknew the day Moses would deliver our people from Egypt, or when our people would return to the Promised Land.

- ✡ Miriam, after giving birth could never have imagined the visitors that she would receive. This was prophesied in Psalms 72:10,11, that kings and world dignitaries would one day bow down and serve Him; *"And let all kings bow down before him, all nations serve him."* The Magi who came that day brought gifts to Miriam and Yosef, and their newborn baby. After traveling a great distance, they confirmed prophecy just by them coming to pay homage to the Messiah. Even Herod's spiritual advisors warned the king of the threat that was born at that time.

- ✡ Because of a dream that God gave Yosef, *Yeshua's* birth fulfilled another prophecy by escaping to Egypt as spoken of in Hosea 11:1, *"When Israel was a child, I loved him, and out of Egypt I called my son."* Then upon receiving word of Herod's death, Yosef and his *Mishpocha* returned to Israel and settled in Nazareth, where He was raised as a Nazarene; *"A shoot will come up from the stump of Jess from his roots a Branch will bear fruit"* (Isaiah 11:1).

YESHUA'S JEWISH TRAINING

Another important fact about *Yeshua* is that He grew up like any other "Jewish" child born to simple observant "Jewish" parents. Yet He had no distinctive characteristics that brought attention to Him at that time. This is an accepted fact in Judaism.

- ✡ One unique characteristic is that He was accepted as a righteous scholar early on. As a young man, He was already respected as a scholar of Torah, and the deep traditions of His people, Israel. As *Yeshua* was preparing for His *Bar Mitzvah,* Miriam and Yosef, brought Him to the *Beit Hamikdash* (Temple) at the time; this was a mitzvah to be fulfilled by all observant Jews. There he would be trained in the Hebrew Scriptures and Jewish practices.

- ✡ *Yeshua*, of course, took it seriously because of His love for G-d. At a young age, He enjoyed discussing with the Rabbi's and religious leaders the scriptures. One writer wrote of Him that, at the age of 12, *"He was wise beyond His years and amazed them at His understanding and breadth of knowledge"* (Luke 2:41-52).

When it came time for *Yeshua* to begin His earthly work to the House of Israel, He went to His cousin Yochanan (John) to undergo Mikvah (immersion). As He was being immersed, *Adonai* spoke over His Son, *"This is my beloved Son in whom I am well pleased."* The *Ruach haCodesh* (Holy Spirit) was seen descending upon *Yeshua*, *"like a dove"* thus immersing him in water and the Spirit, thereby giving Him the blessing to begin to go forth and preach the good news (Matthew 3:16; Mark 1:10).

The fact that He was called a "Son," brings us back to our first statement made earlier in this book; Yeshua is the only human being that is a man and yet G-d at the same time. He came in human form but retained divine character and attributes. We learn from Scripture that he had never sinned even under the most trying and temptation filled times.

No human being has ever lived his life without sin. But only *Maschiach* had the power to refrain from sin in order to live a life of complete obedience to Abba Father. Hence, no other Rabbi, past, or present, has ever lived this way or will do so in the future. On this basis alone, *Maschiach* our Jewish Messiah requires us to search and ask questions. One is compelled! We must ponder the significances of one prophecy upon another and search our Torah for our *Maschiach*!

YESHUA'S WORK

Another unusual aspect of His life is that historically, many were looking for a *Maschiach* who would rule with an iron fist to cleanse the land of paganism and idolatry and drive out the Roman inhabitants of the land. The true Messiah work would take on a different character, one not understood by the Jewish leadership of the day.

- ✡ G-d chose to bring redemption in an unsuspecting way through an unsuspecting vessel. Yet every aspect of His arrival, life, and suffering was a complete fulfillment of the Jewish writings. Yeshayahu, Isaiah, spoke accurately of the Coming One, and that HE would bring *Tikkun O lam* (repair to the world) by healing the broken hearted, opening the blind eyes, bringing hope to the hopeless, and being a light to the Gentiles.

- ✡ For this reason, *Maschiach* would not enter Jerusalem preceded by an army and a cavalry of horses. Only on a lowly donkey with a few at His side would He enter the Holy City of Jerusalem according to the writings of the prophets (Zechariah 9:9). *Yeshua* would preach the good news (essentially the Torah,) and seek and save those that have lost their way from Torah. He predicted that He would begin his ministry work in Galilee, to the very people He came to redeem, and that they would reject Him John 1:11).

- ✡ Throughout, Yeshua spent much of His time teaching in parables as foretold in Tehilim (Psalm 78,) and recorded in Matityahu (Matthew 13). He astounded the leaders of the time with the way He spoke with wisdom and authority. Upon seeing the disgrace of what had become of the Temple court with a market and place of business, *Maschiach* fulfilled another prophecy from Malachi 3 when he purified it from all of the moneychangers, which was is detailed in Matityahu 21.

✡ His grand entrance into *Yerushalayim*, or what Christian tradition observes as Palm Sunday, had throngs of Jewish people greeting Him with psalms and songs of praise (a kingly greeting.) That day when He arrived thousands of Jewish people were busy selecting their special lamb sacrifice for the Passover. If our ancestors had only known the significance of this Lamb, Yeshua, how different would this story be!

✡ His arrival in Jerusalem on a donkey had been registered in Zechariah 9:9, a passage previously noted, centuries before *Maschiach* entered Jerusalem on a donkey. His entire life was about doing Abba Father's work, whether he was preaching the Torah, or teaching the multitudes His wisdom and purpose of coming, (Isaiah 61:48.)

YESHUA'S DEATH & RESURRECTION

Profound no doubt, is *Yeshua's* resurrection. Once again, we find ourselves in the supernatural construct of Jewish Messianism. Something that we cannot escape! No person in history has ever had his entire life predicted to such an extent like *Yeshua's*. Even his death was predicted. When we read the accounts of Messiah betrayal, resurrection, death, and ascension, every detail was foretold centuries before *Yeshua* was even born. Every step of His life on earth unfolded miraculous proof of His Messianic Jewish credentials.

Again, the Jewish prophet Yeshayahu, (Isaiah) in chapter 53:5, states; *"He would be bruised for our inequities and wounded for our sorrows, and the chastisement (punishment) of our peace would be upon Him."* Matityahu, or Matthew's gospel, chronicles Yeshua's entire trial and how He stood silently before his accusers just like Yeshayahu wrote again in chapter 53. In chapter 50:6 Isaiah writes that *"I offered my back to those who beat me, my cheeks to those who pulled out my beard; I did not hide my face from mocking and spitting."* Again in 53, he writes, *"He would be wounded, afflicted and oppressed by His own, and finally taken by force."* In the hour of His greatest need, His Talmidim, disciples, abandoned Him in the garden as foreshadowed by the prophet Zechariah, *"Awake, sword, against my shepherd, against the man who is close to me!" declares the LORD Almighty. "Strike the shepherd, and the sheep will be scattered, and I will turn my hand against the little ones.* (Zechariah 13:7)

Yet, David in Tehilim 22, a scroll dated around 1000BCE, accurately predicted Messiah's death, along with the events that happened during that 6-hour window. In accordance with the Tanakh, *Maschiach* would come to be mocked and flogged. His hands and feet would be bound and pierced. He would be nailed to a wooden stake, or cross, which was the custom of that day. Exactly in accordance with the Jewish writings, His side would be pierced, and vinegar would be offered to quench His thirst. His clothes would be gambled away by those casting lots for it. Throughout His brutal suffering, miraculously, not a bone would be broken. Those closest to Him would watch from afar or from the foot of the cross. The fact that His friends watched from afar is even seen in Psalm 38 and 88. He anguished in His soul over what He was to suffer, yet he was always willing and obedient servant as recorded in Isaiah 50. In the midst of certain death, *Yeshua* always prayed for His persecutors because He was committed to the will of His Abba Father, this so the ultimate plan of redemption can be completed (Psalm 22, 109 and Isaiah 53).

> - Who could do this other than *Yeshua haMashiach*? Only *Yeshua* chose to bear the sins of the world just like Isaiah 53:4 states; *"Surely, he took up our pain and bore our suffering, yet we considered him punished by God, stricken by him, and afflicted."*

> - *Maschiach* was without sin, how else could He become the spotless Lamb that was required in Exodus 12? He alone willingly surrendered His life in exchange for His own people Israel, as well as for the world and for your life today. All of this was done so He could pay the ultimate debt that sin required (Isaiah 53). When many thought it was all over upon His impending death, *Maschiach* quoted the Jewish writings of King David by reciting Psalm 31:5, *"Into your hands I commit my spirit; deliver me,*

LORD, my faithful God." A darkness fell over the land upon His death as prophesied in Psalm 22 and Amos 8, and it seemed like *Yeshua's* ministry had come to an end. But in reality, it had just begun!

IN CONCLUSION: The Messiah had established in <u>one single act</u> the longing and expectations of Judaism. Every recorded detail came from the annals of the Jewish prophets. He, the Jewish Messiah, ratified a new covenant that Jeremiah in chapter 31 speaks of, and also fulfilled Malachi 3. He was Zion's redeemer; Israel's King of Kings in the future. Death could not hold him just like Psalms and Isaiah states. Hence, death was not the end but the beginning. And as many on the mount saw the ascension, all will see His return when He comes in a blaze of glory as Maschiach ben David—King Messiah, son of David!

NOTES:

INDISPUTABLE FACTS

OF THE MESSIAH

The following Old Testament prophecies deal with the authentication of *Maschiach's* credentials as the Jewish Messiah. They were uttered by many different voices over a period of 500 years. Most all of them were fulfilled within twenty-four hours on the day that He died for the sins of the world. Consider the following facts.

[FACT I]

PROPHECY: Maschiach would be betrayed for thirty pieces of silver: Zechariah 11:13, "then the LORD said to me, *"Throw it to the potter, that magnificent price at which they valued me."* So, I took the thirty shekels of silver and threw them to the potter in the house of the LORD.

FULFILLMENT: Matthew 27:5-7 *"And he threw the pieces of silver into the sanctuary and departed, and he went away and hanged himself. And the chief priests took the pieces of silver and said, 'It is not lawful to put them into the temple treasury since it is the price of blood.' And they counseled together and with the money bought the Potter's Field as a burial place for strangers."*

[FACT II]

PROPHECY: *Maschiach* **would be betrayed by a friend.** Psalm 55:12-14, *"for it is not an enemy who reproaches me, then I could bear it; nor is it one who hates me who has exalted himself against me, then I could hide from him. But it is you, a man my equal, my companion and my familiar friend. We who had sweet fellowship together and walked in the house of God in the throng"* (See also Psalm 41:9; Zechariah 13:6).

FULFILLMENT: Matthew 26:49-50, *"and immediately he went to Jesus and said, 'Hail, Rabbi!' and kissed Him. And Yeshua said to him, 'Friend, do what you have come for.' Then they came and laid hands on Jesus and seized Him.'"*

[FACT III]

PROPHECY: Most of *Maschiach's* disciples would forsake Him, then later accept Him. Zechariah 13:7 *"'Awake, O sword, against My Shepherd, and against the man, My Associate,' Declares the LORD of hosts. 'Strike the Shepherd that the sheep may be scattered, And I will turn My hand against the little ones.'"*

FULFILLMENT: Matthew 26:56 *"'But all this has taken place that the Scriptures of the prophets may be fulfilled.' Then all the disciples left Him and fled.'"* (See also Mk. 14:27)

[FACT IV]

PROPHECY: *Maschiach* **would be falsely accused.** Psalm 35:11, *"false witnesses rise; they ask me of things that I do not know."*

FULFILLMENT: Matthew 26:59-60 *"Now the chief priests and the whole council kept trying to obtain false testimony against Yeshua, so that they might put Him to death; and they did not find any, even though many false witnesses came forward."*

[FACT V]

PROPHECY: Maschiach would be smitten and spat upon. Isaiah 50:6, *"I gave My back to those who strike Me, And My cheeks to those who pluck out the beard; I did not cover My face from humiliation and spitting."*

FULFILLMENT: Matthew 27:30, *"And they spat on Him, and took the reed and began to beat Him on the head."*

[FACT VI]

PROPHECY: *Maschiach* **would stand defenseless before his accusers.** Isaiah 53:7, *"He was oppressed, and He was afflicted, Yet He did not open His mouth; Like a lamb that is led to slaughter, and like a sheep that is silent before its shearers, So He did not open His mouth."*

FULFILLMENT: Matthew 27:12-14, *"and while He was being accused by the chief priests and elders, He made no answer. Then Pilate said to Him, 'Do You not hear how many things they testify against You?' And He did not answer him about even a single charge so that the governor was quite amazed."*

[FACT VII]

PROPHECY: *Maschiach* **would be wounded and bruised as "The Passover Lamb."** Isaiah 53:5, *"But He was pierced through for our transgressions, He was crushed for our iniquities; the chastening for our well-being fell upon Him, and by His scourging, we are healed."*

FULFILLMENT: Matthew 27:26, 29, *"then he released Barabbas for them; but after having Jesus scourged, he delivered Him to be crucified. And after weaving a crown of thorns, they put it on His head, and a reed in His right hand; and they kneeled down before Him and mocked Him, saying, 'Hail, King of the Jews!'"*

[FACT VIII]

PROPHECY: *Maschiach* **would bear the full penalty of sin for others.** Isaiah 53:5-6, 8, 12, *"But He was wounded and crushed for our sins. He was beaten that we might have peace. He was whipped, and we were healed! All of us have strayed away like sheep. We have left God's paths to follow our own. Yet the Lord laid on Him the guilt and sins of us all. From prison and trial, they led Him away to His death. But who among the people realized that He was dying for their sins – that He was suffering their punishment? I will give Him the honors of One who is mighty and great because He exposed Himself to death. He was counted among those who were sinners. He bore the sins of many and interceded for sinners."* (See also Psalm 109:24)

FULFILLMENT: John 19:17, *"They took Jesus therefore, and He went out, bearing His own cross, to the place called the Place of a Skull, which is called in Hebrew, Golgotha."*

Luke 23:26, *"And when they led Him away, they laid hold of one Simon of Cyrene, coming in from the country, and placed on him the cross to carry behind Jesus."*

[FACT IX]

PROPHECY: During his suffering, *Maschiach's* hands and feet would be Pierced. Psalm 22:16, *"For dogs have surrounded me; A band of evildoers has encompassed me; they pierced my hands and my feet."*

FULFILLMENT: Luke 23:33 *"And when they came to the place called The Skull, there they crucified Him and the criminals, one on the right and the other on the left."*

[FACT X]

PROPHECY: *Maschiach* would suffer capital punishment and be crucified with thieves. Isaiah 53:12, *"Therefore, I will allot Him a portion with the great, And He will divide the booty with the strong; Because He poured out Himself to death, and was numbered with the transgressors, Yet He bore the sin of many and interceded for the transgressors."*

FULFILLMENT: Mark 15:27-28, *"And they crucified two robbers with Him, one on His right and one on His left. And the Scripture was fulfilled which says, "And He was numbered with transgressors."*

[FACT XI]

PROPHECY: *Maschiach* would bear the sin of his persecutors and intercede on their behalf. Isaiah 53:12, *"Therefore, I will allot Him a portion with the great, And He will divide the body with the strong; Because He poured out Himself to death and was numbered with the transgressors."*

FULFILLMENT: Luke 23:34, *"But Jesus was saying, 'Father, forgive them; for they do not know what they are doing.' And they cast lots, dividing up His garments among themselves."*

[FACT XII]

PROPHECY: The crowds would shake their heads in disdain, and bewilderment for *Maschiach*. Psalm 109:25, *"I also have become a reproach to them; when they see me, they wag their head."*

FULFILLMENT: Matthew 27:39, *"And those passing by were hurling abuse at Him, wagging their heads."*

[FACT XIII]

PROPHECY: *Maschiach* would be ridiculed by many. Psalm 22:7-8, *"But I am a worm and not a man, scorned by men and despised by the people. All who see me mock me, they hurl insults, shaking their heads."*

FULFILLMENT: Matthew 27:41-43 "In the same way the chief priests also, along with the scribes and elders, were mocking Him, and saying, 'He saved others; He cannot save Himself. He is the King of Israel; let Him now come down from the cross, and we shall believe in Him. He trusts in God; let Him deliver Him now if He takes pleasure in Him;' for He said, 'I am the Son of God.'"

[FACT XIV]

PROPHECY: Immediately upon *Maschiach's* death His garments would be torn apart and divided. Psalm 22:18, *"They divide my garments among them and for my clothing they cast lots."*

FULFILLMENT: John 19:23-24, *"The soldiers, therefore, when they had crucified Jesus, took His outer garments and made four parts, a part to every soldier and also the tunic; now the tunic was seamless, woven in one piece. They said therefore to one another, 'Let us not tear it, but cast lots for it, to decide whose it shall be,' that the Scripture might be fulfilled; 'They divided My outer garments among them, and for My clothing they cast lots."*

[FACT XV]

PROPHECY: *Maschiach* **would feel separation from His Abba Father.** Psalm 22:1, *"A Psalm of David. My God, my God, why hast Thou forsook me? Far from my deliverance are the words of my groaning."*

FULFILLMENT: Matthew 27:46, *"and about the ninth hour Jesus cried out with a loud voice, saying, 'Eli, Eli, lama sabachthani?' That is, 'My God, My God, why hast Thou forsook me?'"*

[FACT XVI]

PROPHECY: Gall and vinegar would be given to *Maschiach* **while He Hung on the Cross.** Psalm 69:21, *"they also gave me gall for my food, and for my thirst they gave me vinegar to drink."*

FULFILLMENT: John 19:28-29, *"After this, Jesus, knowing that all things had already been accomplished, so that the Scripture might be fulfilled, said, 'I am thirsty.' A jar full of sour wine was standing there; so, they put a sponge full of the sour wine upon a branch of hyssop and brought it up to His mouth."*

[FACT XVII]

PROPHECY: *Maschiach* **would always be committed to God.** Psalm 31:5, *"Into Thy hand I commit my spirit; Thou hast ransomed me, O LORD, God of truth."*

FULFILLMENT: Luke 23:46, *"And Jesus, crying out with a loud voice, said, "Father, into Thy hands, I commit My spirit." And having said this, He breathed His last."*

[FACT XVIII]

PROPHECY: Not one bone of *Maschiach's* **body would be broken.** Psalm 34:20, *"He keeps all his bones; Not one of them is broken."*

FULFILLMENT: John 19:33, 36, *"but coming to Jesus, when they saw that He was already dead, they did not break His legs; For these things came to pass, that the Scripture might be fulfilled," Not a bone of Him shall be broken."*

[FACT XIX]

PROPHECY: *Maschiach's* **side would be pierced.** Zechariah 12:10, *"And I will pour out on the house of David and on the inhabitants of Jerusalem, the Spirit of grace and of supplication, so that they will look on Me whom they have pierced; and they will mourn for Him as one mourns for an only son, and they will weep bitterly over Him, like the bitter weeping over a first-born."*

FULFILLMENT: John 19:34-37, *"but one of the soldiers pierced His side with a spear, and immediately there came out blood and water. And he who has seen has borne witness, and his witness is true, and he knows that he is telling the truth so that you also may believe. For these things came to pass, that the Scripture might be fulfilled, 'not a bone of Him shall be broken.' And again, another Scripture says, 'They shall look on Him whom they pierced."*

[FACT XX]

PROPHECY: Darkness would come over the land upon His death. Amos 8:9 *"'And it will come about in that day,'" declares the Lord GOD, 'That I shall make the sun go down at noon and make the earth dark in broad daylight.'"*

FULFILLMENT: Matthew 27:45 *"Now from the sixth-hour darkness fell upon all the land until the ninth hour."*

[FACT XXI]

PROPHECY: *Maschiach* **would be buried in a rich man's tomb.** Isaiah 53:9, *"His grave was assigned with wicked men, yet He was with a rich man in His death, because He had done no violence, nor was there any deceit in His mouth."*

FULFILLMENT: Matthew 27:57-60, *"And when it was evening, there came a rich man from Arimathea, named Joseph, who himself had also become a disciple of Jesus. This man went to Pilate and asked for the body of Jesus. Then Pilate ordered it to be given over to him. And Joseph took the body and wrapped it in a clean linen cloth, and laid it in his own new tomb, which he had hewn out in the rock; and he rolled a large stone against the entrance of the tomb and went away."*

SECTION XII

SALVATION PRAYER / FINAL CONVERSATION WITH A JEWISH PERSON

Perhaps you have seen for the first time the wealth of prophetic writings that took place thousands of years prior to our Messiah's coming. Hopefully, you have noticed the incredible weight of evidence that is presented in both the Old and later Jewish writings (New Testament) that speak about the Messiah. The fact that you have taken the time to listen and review it speaks to your inquiring heart and mind. Already G-d is perhaps speaking to your heart regarding the Messiah. It may seem like a difficult concept for you as a Jewish person to believe in Jesus, or in Hebrew *Yeshua*. But it is not contrary to the Torah, or the hundreds of thousands of Jewish people that receive Him today, and the thousands that accepted Him two thousand years ago. With hundreds of prophecies and fulfillments of Messiah in our *Tanakh*, believing in *Yeshua* became for me the most Jewish decision that any Jewish person can make. You can also experience this! Simply, from the depth and sincerity of your heart, you can receive Him.

As the prophet, Jeremiah in chapter 31 spoke of; God would write His law upon our hearts and minds. No longer would we need to go to our Rabbi's and ask about the meaning of these words. We would simply need to ask G-d to open our heart and mind to the truth of our Messiah. Recall these words from our Scriptures that are found in 1 Chronicles 15:2, *"The Lord is with you when you are with him. If you seek him, he will be found by you.* Finally, offer to the God of Abraham, Isaiah, and Jacob, the same God whom we believe in, this simple prayer:

PRAYER — PRAYING WITH A JEWISH PERSON:

Adonai, I thank you for your love. I thank you that You have never changed from the days of our people in the wilderness to the deliverances that have preserved us. As you led our people through the dry wilderness and into the Promised Land thousands of years ago, you have ensured our survival; You have given us our covenant land; our Torah, our Messiah. And as prophesied by our prophets, You Father sent *Yeshua* to be my final Passover sacrificial lamb that I might receive life, truth, hope, and strength. Through Him, I may be restored to a personal and life-giving relationship with my Abba Father.

Abba, I receive Your gift of life through your Son, *Yeshua,* as my Messiah. I recognize now that He came and died for me, that you may forgive me of my sins through my Messiah. I ask that You, *Yeshua,* reach into my heart and take loving hold of my life so that I may live as my Abba Father designed for me. Lord, I ask that you become my King and Savior. Help me to live for you and be your child.

A WORD FROM DR. MITCH GLASER
DIRECTOR OF CHOSEN PEOPLE MINISTRIES

The Apostle John gives a good summary of witnessing in his first epistle: "the life [of Jesus] was manifested, and we have seen, and bear witness, and declare to you . . . that which we have seen and heard . . ." (1 John 1:2-3). Effective witnessing is telling what one has seen and/or heard-much as a witness in a legal case gives a testimony. But witnessing to a Jewish person goes far beyond reciting the facts of the Gospel message. Witnessing must become a dialogue between two individuals, each with mutual respect and a genuine interest in the well-being of the other. Because the best witness is the witness of a friend or close relation (see John 1:40-45), the first step in sharing the Gospel with a Jewish person is to develop a friendship. Your witness will do best as it grows naturally out of a deepening relationship.

Don't befriend a Jewish person merely to "get him saved," however. The person will sense this and feel you are only interested in him as a project or trophy. Let your friendship and love be genuine. It must not rise or fall on your friend's response to the Gospel. Witnessing encounters with strangers are certainly wonderful opportunities, but this pamphlet describes a witness that takes place within the context of a growing relationship. (And, for editorial efficiency, this pamphlet uses "him" to refer to the person to whom you may be witnessing about the person of Jesus.)

Try to understand your Jewish friend. It is important to understand your Jewish friend's mindset towards the Gospel message. What is to you a beautifully clear story of redemption actually presents several deep-rooted obstacles to your Jewish friend. Here are a few simple points that can help you be more sensitive:

Have you noticed that Jewish people are frequently negative towards Christianity? You might be too if your people had been persecuted over the centuries in "Christian countries" and in the name of Christ! Many Jewish person believe that to become a Christian is to side with those who have mistreated his people. This is tantamount to treachery to one's ancestors.

- Jewish people cannot comprehend how a person can be a Jew and a Christian at the same time. They presume that if they accept Jesus they can no longer be Jewish.

- Jewish people are not especially religious. Most modern Jews value the traditional and cultural elements of their heritage more than the religious. In fact, synagogue attendance in the United States is below 15%!
- Jewish people are taught to reject certain essential teachings of the Bible such as the Trinity, the deity of the Messiah, and the Second Coming of Jesus.
- Jewish people are not especially familiar with the Old Testament. Most would question whether the Bible was even inspired by God. Orthodox Jews do accept the Scriptures, but most modern and secular Jewish people do not accept the divine authority of their own Old Testament.
- Most Jewish people are surprised to hear that Jesus was Jewish and the New Testament was written by Jews. They view the New Testament as a "non-Jewish" book that has spawned another world religion. Some even think Jesus was a nice Jewish boy who converted to Christianity!
- Jewish people intuitively know that if they were to consider Jesus, their families and friends would not understand them, and some might even disown them. We see an example of this in John 9, where the Jewish leaders threatened the parents of the blind man with excommunication if they acknowledged that Jesus had healed their son.

Your Jewish friend might have other objections to the Gospel as well. He might be an agnostic or even an atheist. He might not believe in God or even in the coming of the Messiah. Before you present the Gospel, you might need to begin by establishing evidence about the existence of God and the reliability of the Bible. Besides these, particularly Jewish dynamics in witnessing, don't forget that Scripture declares that ". . . There is none who seeks after God" (Romans 3:11). No human being, apart from the intervention of the Holy Spirit, seeks to admit his need for salvation before a holy God. So, don't let an initial rejection discourage you. Anticipate the first "no," but then keep looking for opportunities to extend God's love and patiently share the Gospel.

BIBLICAL PRINCIPLES OF WITNESSING

1. USE THE BIBLE: The Scriptures tell us that faith comes through hearing the Word of God (see Romans 10:17). Sometimes, because Jewish people are not familiar with the New Testament or even with the Old, we tend to use reason and logic more than God's Word. The Bible has self-authenticating authority that can touch hearts: "So shall My word be that goes forth from My mouth; it shall not return to Me void, but it shall accomplish what I please, and it shall prosper in the thing for which I sent it" (Isaiah 55:11). The Scriptures should be the key benchmark of truth when we are witnessing.

2. PRESENT A PERSON: Don't be discouraged when your friend rejects Christianity. There is often much historical baggage involved. Just remember: The Gospel is about a Person-Jesus the Messiah. It is about a relationship, not a religion. When you distinguish between Jesus and the Jewish understanding of the Christian religion, many objections dissipate. Your Jewish friend does not need to feel that by accepting Jesus he is giving up his Jewish identity. You are not asking him to "convert" to another religion, but to become "complete" by receiving the Jewish Messiah.

3. WATCH YOUR LANGUAGE: Certain words may have totally different, even offensive, meanings to your Jewish friend. Often, such words as "cross" and "Christ" bring up collective memories of persecution by so-called "Christians." Be sensitive in your choice of words. Try using "Messiah" instead of "Christ," "tree" instead of "cross," and even "Yeshua" instead of "Jesus." You want to communicate the Jewishness of the Gospel message.

4. BE A CREDIBLE WITNESS: A witness declares what he or she has seen and heard. Although you have not seen or spoken with Messiah Jesus on this earth (as did the Apostle John), you can still be a credible witness to the life-changing reality of His presence in your life. This is not so much by your verbal witness but by the witness of your life, demonstrating that the Messiah lives in and through you. In other words, witnesses should only testify about what they personally know to be true.

Some ice-breakers can help you get started. Some of the best opportunities about the Lord happen during normal, friendly interactions. Don't be afraid of offending your Jewish friend by bringing up the subject of your faith in Jesus.

5. AFFIRM YOUR FRIEND'S JEWISH IDENTITY: By affirming your friend's Jewish identity, you will be showing your love for him and making the statement that he can be Jewish and believe in Jesus! You can do this tactfully by sending greeting cards on the Jewish holidays, showing an interest in current events that concern the Jewish people and especially by showing some sensitivity to what is happening in Israel.

Many of the Jewish holidays, such as Passover and the Fall Feasts, appear in the New Testament and can give you an opportunity to present the Gospel. Your friend will be intrigued that your belief in Jesus gives you an appreciation for Jewish heritage. Chosen People Ministries has materials available to help you be a more effective witness by incorporating a spiritual understanding of the Jewish holidays.

6. SHARE YOUR TESTIMONY: Tell your Jewish friend that you believe in the Jewish Messiah, and then tell him what Jesus has done for you! This will be especially powerful if you are a Gentile and have accepted the Lord as an adult. Showing how even a Gentile needed to accept Jesus will counter the idea that Christians are simply "born into the religion." Your friend may realize for the first time that this relationship is entered into by faith and not merely by birth. Go ahead and tell him that God did not make you stop being Italian, Norwegian or Oklahoman, and that he doesn't have to stop being Jewish!

7. LOOK FOR AN AREA OF NEED: Your Jewish friend might tell you about a problem. This is the time to bring up an appropriate Scripture or even to pray for him. Perhaps you can suggest a Christian book that addresses the problem. Let him know ahead of time that the book is written from a Christian perspective, so that there are no surprises. Follow up later to get his opinion on the book's contents.

Invite your friend to church. Don't be afraid of inviting your Jewish friend to a special event at church that might interest him - perhaps a special speaker, video series, or musical event. You can offer to attend synagogue in return. Just the act of inviting him may open up opportunities to share your faith.

8. ASK DIRECT QUESTIONS: You might find that jumping in and asking thoughtful questions works for you. Here are some ideas:
- As a Jewish person, how do you practice your religion?
- How often do you read the Bible? What role does it play in your life?
- What do you believe about the Messiah?

9. INTRODUCE YOUR FRIEND TO A JEWISH BELIEVER: Another way to tell your Jewish friend about Jesus is to introduce him to Jewish believers. There are many ways to do this. You can contact Metro Jewish Resources, or Chosen People Ministries, as we are in touch with a worldwide network of Jewish people who believe in Jesus, many of whom would be more than willing to meet your Jewish friend.

> *We can also tell you about Messianic meetings in various areas, so you can accompany your Jewish friend to a Bible study or service that is Jewish in character, where of course Jesus is lifted up as Messiah and Savior. If you cannot take advantage of these opportunities, you can still introduce your friend to Jewish believers through written testimonies. There are many ways to make it clear to your Jewish friends that your hope for them is to enter into a relationship with the living God through Jesus the Messiah. You are not trying to convert them to another religion! By God's grace, your Jewish friend will see that belief in Jesus is the most Jewish belief he can have!

10. PRESENTING THE GOSPEL FROM THE HEBREW SCRIPTURES: Once you establish a friendship, and are sensitive to your Jewish friend's special needs, you can present the Gospel in a number of different ways. There is no "right" or "wrong" way. After all, you are not witnessing to "the Jews," but to an individual Jewish person who has ideas, needs, and personal thoughts and questions about the meaning of life.

11. STUDY THE GOSPELS: It's always a good idea to encourage your friend to read the Bible on his own. If your friend is interested in studying the Bible with you, a good place to begin is the Gospel of Matthew, which was written especially to the Jewish people. In Matthew, he will not only see Jesus as the Messiah, but will discover many Old Testament passages about the Messiah which Matthew quotes (at least 47 references, most of them Messianic). You might also try the Gospel of John, as it will enable your friend to grapple with the teachings of Jesus. When you study the Gospels with your Jewish friend, be sure to go slowly, explaining the meaning of unfamiliar theological terms. Go back to the Old Testament when the Gospel writers quote it. Be sensitive to the Jewish issues involved - the controversies with Jewish leaders, the celebration of Jewish holidays. Point out how Jewish the New Testament really is!

✡ **STUDY MESSIANIC PROPHECY:** Another good way to study is to review Old Testament Messianic prophecy-which paints a picture of the Messiah-and then look to the New Testament for the fulfillment of those prophecies. Remember, your Jewish friend is beginning his study with little background, even in the Old Testament. Begin with some of the major Messianic prophecies. Try to point out the context of the passages and allow your friend to discover many of the truths for himself. Ask questions as you go over the text. Let your friend read the passage and see if he can answer some questions you ask of the text. "To what does the prophet refer?" "Who fits that description?" These questions will help your Jewish friend grapple with the text and come to his own conclusions.

APPENDIX I

THE KINGDOM

- ✡ **RESTORE ORDER:** The first order of events upon the advent of the Kingdom of Heaven is an immediate restoration of righteous government and order for all mankind as well as creation.

- ✡ **NO MORE INFANT MORTALITY:** Isaiah 65:20, *"No longer will there be an infant who lives but a few days or an old man who does not live out his days; for the youth will die at the age of one hundred and be considered accursed."* Meaning, every person, young and old, will have the ability to live for 1,000 years and beyond without sickness, except for those that commit some death penalty sin.

- ✡ **FEASTS RESTORED:** Succoth, or Tabernacles, is seen in Zechariah 14.18. *"If the family of Egypt does not go up or enter, then no rain will fall on them; it will be the plague with which the LORD smites the nations that do not go up to celebrate the Feast of Booths."* This will be the punishment of Egypt, and the punishment of all the nations who do not go up to celebrate the Feast of Booths.

- ✡ **RIGHTEOUS GOVERNMENT RETURNS:** Isaiah 32.1, *"See, a king will reign in righteousness, and rulers will rule with justice."*

- ✡ **NATIONS RETURN TO THEIR GOD GIVEN BORDERS:** Deuteronomy 32:8, *"when the Most High gave the nations their inheritance when he divided all mankindd, he set up boundaries for the peoples according to the number of the sons of Israel."* Not only will Israel's original borders be restored, but the nations will return to their original borders as well.

- ✡ **RIGHTEOUS RULING CITIES:** Matthew 25:21, *"Well done, my good servant!' his master replied. 'Because you have been trustworthy in small things, take charge of ten cities.'"*

- ✡ **PATRIARCHS RETURN** Matthew 8:11, *"I say to you that many will come from the east and the west and will take their places at the feast with Abraham, Isaiah, and Jacob in the kingdom of heaven."*

- ✡ **NATURE TRANSFORMED:** Immediately a complete reversal of the predatory spirit will release nature from chaos and contention; the lion will eat straw like the ox and lay next to the Lamb. [xlii]

- ✡ **ONE FAITH ONE RELIGION:** Those long turned off to religion will at last find godly solidarity, as one faith, one Messiah, and one devout system will exist. Every nation and tongue will worship the Lord God of Abraham, Isaiah, and Jacob.

- ✡ **NEW ORDER ON EARTH: A New Order will exist upon the earth, one in Hebraic Structure and the perfect government will take hold.** Mourning will give way to joy, as death will give way to life, and war will give way to peace. Humankind will finally experience on the earth a time of honest government and rulers, as the human government will yield to the moral rule of the Messianic kingdom.[xliii] With political genocide and ethnic cleansing of a past age, everyone will live in divine health. Special trees will be grown whose leaves will have healing powers for the nations.[xliv]

- ✡ **ISRAEL'S FINAL RETURN:** One of the goals of the 1000-year earthly kingdom of Christ will be to vindicate His chosen people Israel before the eyes of all nations. [xlv]Though the Jewish people have been a persecuted people, scattered, for thousands of generations, everyone will learn the reason for such a long-suffering upon a specific people. Before this takes place, however, a judgment will take place, which was noted earlier called *"the sheep and goat judgment in the Valley of Jehoshaphat."* [xlvi] There the goat nations, those that sided with the anti-Christ and persecuted the Jewish people) during the Great Tribulation will be judged. [xlvii]

Something else will occur. A fourth temple will be built! Yes, before God's plan reaches its climax the Jewish people build a third Temple. This will take place sometime before The Great Tribulation this will begin to be built. But when it is completed it will be destroyed again as the former two. This last one, however, will take place at the hands of the anti-Christ and his armies. There will also be a fourth and final Temple that is portrayed in Ezekiel's writings in chapters 40-48. The Prophet speaks with great detail about a Temple that is perhaps much larger than any one before it. Scriptures about various tribulation passages foresee a reshaping of this geographical area due to earthquakes and other events.

- In the Millennial Kingdom, the earth will finally be cleansed from all former denominational streams, man-made doctrines, religious orders, and the age-old teaching of replacement theology. The words of Isaiah and the Psalms become a reality: "For out of Zion shall go forth the law and the word of the Lord from Jerusalem" (Isaiah 2:3, NKJV). *"If I forget thee, O Jerusalem, let my right hand forget her cunning. If I do not remember thee, let my tongue cleave to the roof of my mouth; if I prefer not Jerusalem above my chief joy"* (Psalm 137:5–6 KJV).

- ✡ **RESTORED GOVERNMENT:** A vital connection remains to be discovered between the administration of God's Kingdom and the Jewish people. First, government is always a component to God's blueprint for His Kingdom. Peter's actions highlighted this when he sought to replace Judas one of the twelve in Acts 1:25–26. Why could they not proceed with the eleven? Well, it's simple! A governmental formula was needed; twelve apostles must rule over the twelve tribes of Israel following Israel's full and national regeneration. The principle of government is also illustrated in the ascension gifts that *Yeshua* gave before He [xlviii] ascended. He gave **Apostles, Prophets, Evangelists, Pastors,** and **Teachers.** All were given to maintain order (Eph. 4:9–14).

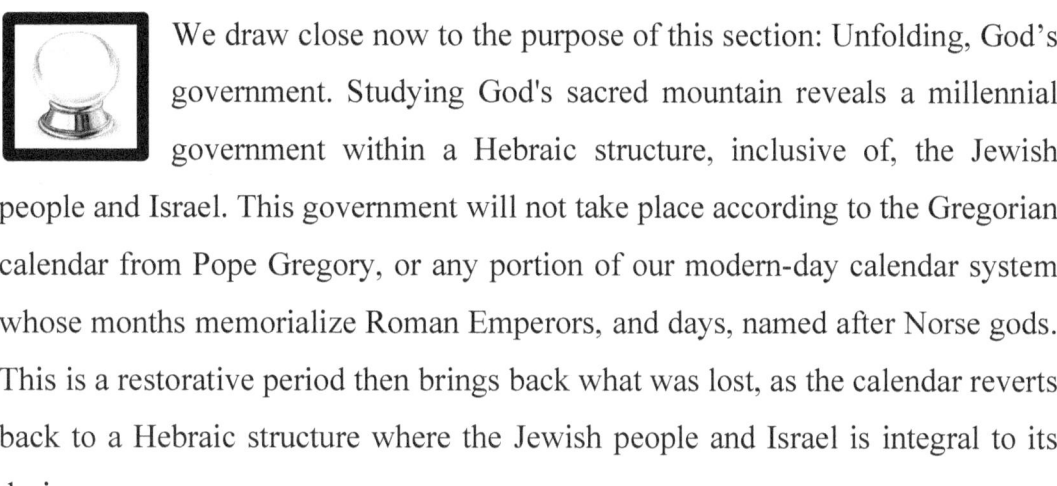

We draw close now to the purpose of this section: Unfolding, God's government. Studying God's sacred mountain reveals a millennial government within a Hebraic structure, inclusive of, the Jewish people and Israel. This government will not take place according to the Gregorian calendar from Pope Gregory, or any portion of our modern-day calendar system whose months memorialize Roman Emperors, and days, named after Norse gods. This is a restorative period then brings back what was lost, as the calendar reverts back to a Hebraic structure where the Jewish people and Israel is integral to its design.

✡ **END TIME RESURRECTION:** Resurrections were always associated with significant advances of the kingdom: *"The tombs broke open, and the bodies of many holy people were raised to life" (Matthew 27:52).* In the future, the biblical forefathers will return via the same way to provide every nation an opportunity to sit down with them in Jerusalem.

- One can only imagine this future time when every living soul is worshiping together at the Feast of Tabernacles (Zechariah 14:6). Daniel speaks pointedly of a resurrection in chapter's eleven and twelve in the last three verses. He deals with the redemption of Israel: *"And many of them that sleep in the dust of the earth shall awake, some to everlasting life, and some to reproaches and everlasting abhorrence"* (Daniel 12:2). Daniel does not say all of them, but many of them that have fallen asleep will return to usher in a Davidic order on the earth. This is a fascinating look into this future time.

- Specifically, after the three and a half years of the tribulation, he is told to wait an additional forty-five days. These totals 1,335 days from the abomination in the temple.

- Daniel is assured that he and all the Old Testament saints will have a vital part in the kingdom to come; *"for the words are closed up and sealed until the time of the end. Many shall be purified, and made white, and tried; however, the wicked shall do wickedly: and none of the wicked shall understand, but the wise shall understand. And from the time that the daily sacrifice shall be taken away, and the abomination that maketh desolate setup, there shall be a thousand two hundred and ninety days. Blessed is he that waiteth, and cometh to the thousand three hundred and five and thirty days. But go thou thy way till the end be: for thou shalt rest and stand in thy lot at the end of the days"* (Daniel 12:9–13).

- To look out from this summit then, the Messianic kingdom, we discover that all the faithful men and women of old did not lose their calling when they were laid to rest. All the people mentioned in Hebrews 11 and more will return. And again, Jews and Gentiles will serve together in their distinction functioning in their God-given distinct offices. The Talmud describes an end time resurrection this way: *"If the womb, which receives in silence, yet brings forth amid great cries of jubilation, then the grave, which receives the dead amid cries of grief, will much more so bring them forth amid great cries of joy"* (Sanhedrin 92a).

✡ **THE CORRUPTIBLE AND INCORRUPTIBLE:** This topic alone is an extraordinary study. To realize in our mind's eye that *incorruptible* saints will rule *corruptible* earthly kings and people is difficult to capture in our mind's eye. But at last, it will be a time when the earth will be returned to the family of God, which all creation has been groaning for.

- You see, ever since the fall of man, corruptible governments and rulers have ruled over the righteous. God's plan was for the righteous to rule the unrighteous! Also, these forthcoming corruptible individuals are under the authority of the incorruptible saints, come out from the judgment that takes place in the *"Valley of Jehoshaphat.*[xlix] *These have been allowed to enter the Messianic kingdom because they have received the Lord during the Great Tribulation. This will be discussed further as we proceed."*

1. The former King David will return to reign over Israel as Prince. (Isaiah 11:1; 1 Chronicles 22:8–10).

2. The Twelve Apostles will be resurrected to rule over the 12 tribes of Israel.

3. The Biblical calendar will be restored, and people will follow the Biblical feasts, Zechariah.

4. Jerusalem will be the center of the world; *Yeshua* will have His throne on the Temple Mount.

5. Finally, nations will come to Jerusalem to worship and give glory to God.

6. Once *Yeshua* is King, leaders of other nations will look to him for guidance, (Isaiah 2:4).

7. All Israelites will be returned to their homeland, (Isaiah 11:12, Zechariah 10:6).

8. God will seek to destroy all the nations that go against Jerusalem, (Zechariah 12:9, Isaiah 60:12).

9. Israel and Judah will be made into one nation again. (Zechariah 11:12-14, Ezekiel 37:16-22).

10. The Jewish people will experience eternal joy and gladness, (Isaiah 51:11).

11. Nations will recognize the wrongs they did to Israel, (Isaiah 52:13–53:5).

12. The peoples of the world will turn to the Jews for spiritual guidance, (Zechariah 8:23).

13. The ruined cities of Israel will be restored, (Ezekiel 16:55).

14. Weapons of war destroyed, (Ezekiel 39:9).

15. The Temple will be rebuilt, (Ezekiel 40) and will resume many of the suspended commandments.

16. He, *Yeshua*, will perfect the entire world; Jew and Gentile will serve God together, (Zephaniah 3:9).

17. *Yeshua* will take the barren land and make it abundant and fruitful, (Isaiah 51:3; Amos 9:13–15; Ezekiel 36:29–30; Isaiah 11:6–9). *"The wolf will live with the lamb, the leopard will lie down with the goat, the calf and the lion and the yearling together; and a little child will lead them. The cow will feed with the bear, their young will lie down together, and the lion will eat straw like the ox. The infant will play near the hole of the cobra, and the young child put his hand into the viper's nest. They will neither harm nor destroy on all my holy mountain, for the earth will be full of the knowledge of the Lord as the waters cover the sea,"* (Isaiah 11:6-9).

18. Righteous Judges and counselors will be restored, (Isaiah 1:26).

19. The whole world will worship the One True God of Israel, (Isaiah 2:11-17).

20. Knowledge of God will fill the world. (Isaiah 11:9; Hab. 2).

21. *Yeshua* will be a messenger of peace, (Isaiah 52:7).

In the kingdom to come, all control will finally flow down from our righteous King to the incorruptible saints. Those earthly and corruptible people that have endured the time of Jacobs's trouble will inhabit the earth.[1] The corruptible will dwell with the incorruptible—material and spiritual for a period of one thousand years.

An important principle pertains to the government in the Messianic kingdom: Any time corruptible flesh is on the earth government is required. Therefore, governing those coming out of the former age, the sheep Gentiles that were judged in the "Valley of Jehoshaphat," (Matthew 25:31–46), will be necessary. With corruptible people, still present then, rebellion eventually creeps in.

One place this is demonstrated is in the book of Zechariah. There we learn, that individual nations will be commanded to attend the Feast of Tabernacles in Jerusalem during the Messianic age. Now grasp the brevity of their disobedience; it will take place while Messiah Himself will be reigning on the earth in Jerusalem (Zechariah 14:16–21). Recall, in this period of time, *Yeshua* as the world's Messiah will no longer be someone's theory or opinion, because He will be sitting upon His throne in the Millennial Temple in Jerusalem, as He takes His place as King over the entire earth. Why anyone would rebel against God during this time is mystifying to say the least, as the greatest revelation since the Garden era will exist on the earth, but they will!

APPENDIX II

WIFE OF JEHOVAH PASSAGES

✡ **THE MARRIAGE:** Ezekiel 16:8, "Later I passed by, and when I looked at you and saw that you were old enough for love, I spread the corner of my garment over you and covered your nakedness. I gave you my solemn oath and entered into a covenant with you, declares the Sovereign LORD, and you became mine." (also, Deuteronomy 6:13-15)

✡ **THE GREAT ADULTERY:** Hosea 2:2-5, *"Rebuke your mother, rebuke her, for she is not my wife, and I am not her husband. Let her remove the adulterous look from her face and the unfaithfulness from between her breasts. Otherwise, I will strip her naked and make her as bare as on the day she was born; I will make her like a desert, turn her into a parched land, and slay her with thirst. I will not show my love her children because they are the children of adultery. Their mother has been unfaithful and has conceived them in disgrace.* NIV [11].

✡ **THE SEPARATION:** Isaiah 50:1, *"This is what the LORD says: 'Where is your mother's certificate of divorce with which I sent her away? Or to which of my creditors did I sell you? Because of your sins you were sold; because of your transgressions your mother was sent away.'"* NIV

✡ **THE GREAT DIVORCE:** Jeremiah 3:6-10, *"During the reign of King Josiah, the LORD said to me, 'Have you seen what faithless Israel has done? She has gone up on every high hill and under every spreading tree and has committed adultery there. I thought that after she had done all this, she would return to me, but she did not, and her unfaithful sister Judah saw it. I gave faithless Israel her certificate of divorce and*

---

[11] Further passages: Jeremiah 3:1-5,20; 31:32; Ezekiel 16:15-34

sent her away because of all her adulteries. Yet I saw that her unfaithful sister Judah had no fear; she also went out and committed adultery. Because Israel's immorality Matthewered so little to her, she defiled the land and committed adultery with stone and wood. In spite of all this, her unfaithful sister Judah did not return to me with all her heart, but only in pretense,' declares the LORD." NIV

✡ **THE GREAT PUNISHMENT:** Ezekiel 16:35-43, *"Therefore, you prostitute, hear the word of the LORD! This is what the Sovereign LORD says: 'Because you poured out your wealth and exposed your nakedness in your promiscuity with your lovers, and because of all your detestable idols, and because you gave them your children's blood, therefore I am going to gather all your lovers, with whom you found pleasure, those you loved as well as those you hated. I will gather them against you from all around and will strip you in front of them, and they will see all your nakedness. I will sentence you to the punishment of women who commit adultery and who shed blood; I will bring upon you the blood vengeance of my wrath and jealous anger. Then I will hand you over to your lovers, and they will tear down your mounds and destroy your lofty shrines. They will strip you of your clothes and take your fine jewelry and leave you naked and bare. They will bring a mob against you, who will stone you and hack you to pieces with their swords. They will burn down your houses and inflict punishment on you in the sight of many women. I will put a stop to your prostitution, and you will no longer pay your lovers. Then my wrath against you will subside and my jealous anger will turn away from you; I will be calm and no longer angry. Because you did not remember the days of your youth but enraged me with all these things, I will surely bring down on your head what you have done, declares the Sovereign LORD. Did you not add lewdness to all your other detestable practices?'"* NIV[12]

✡ **THE GREAT REMARRIAGE AND RESTORED BLESSINGS:** Ezekiel 16:60-63, *"Yet I will remember the covenant I made with you in the days of your youth, and I will*

---

[12] Hosea 2:6-13

establish an everlasting covenant with you. Then you will remember your ways and be ashamed when you receive your sisters, both those who are older than you and those who are younger. I will give them to you as daughters, but not on the basis of my covenant with you. So, I will establish my covenant with you, and you will know that I am the LORD. Then, when I make atonement for you for all you have done, you will remember and be ashamed and never again open your mouth because of your humiliation, declares the Sovereign LORD.'" NIV[13]

---

[13] Isaiah 54:1-8; 62:4-5; Hosea 2:14-23

APPENDIX III

MORE BLESSINGS TO THE GENTILES

✡ **GREAT MOUNTAIN WILL BE GIVEN AND ESTABLISHED FOR THE SAKE OF THE NATIONS:** *"In the last days the mountain of the Lord's temple will be established as chief among the mountains; it will be raised above the hills, and all nations will stream to it. Many peoples will come and say, "Come, let us go up to the mountain of the LORD, to the house of the God of Jacob. He will teach us his ways, so that we may walk in his paths. The law will go out from Zion, the word of the LORD from Jerusalem. He will judge between the nations and will settle disputes for many peoples—They will beat their swords into plowshares and their spears into" pruning hooks...nation will not take up sword against nation, nor will they train for war anymore"* Isaiah 2:2-4.

✡ **A SOURCE OF REST FOR THE NATIONS:** *"In that day the Root of Jesse will stand as a banner for the peoples; the nations will rally to him, and his place of rest will be glorious."* Isaiah 11:10.

✡ **SPECIAL BANQUET FOR THE GENTILES:** *"On this mountain, the LORD Almighty will prepare a feast of rich food for all peoples, a banquet of aged wine – the best of meats and the finest of wines"* Isaiah 25:6.

✡ **THE NATIONS WILL FINALLY HAVE SPIRITUAL EYES:** *"On this holy mountain he will destroy the shroud that enfolds all peoples, the sheet that covers all nations"* Isaiah 25:7.

✡ **JUSTICE WILL FINALLY BE BROUGHT TO THE NATIONS:** *"Here is my servant whom I uphold, my chosen one in whom I delight; I will put my Spirit on him, and he will bring justice to the nations"* Isaiah 42:1.

✡ **THE NATIONS WILL BE DRAWN TO SEE THE BLESSED SEED OF GOD:** *"And their seed shall be known among the Gentiles, and their offspring among the people: all *that see them shall acknowledge them, that they are the seed which the LORD hath blessed"* Isaiah 61:9.

✡ **THE NATIONS WILL DRAWN TO THE LIGHT OF JERUSALEM:** *"And the Gentiles shall come to thy light, and kings to the bright- ness of thy rising. Lift up thine eyes round about, and see: all they gather themselves together, they come to thee."* Isaiah 60:3-4.

✡ **THE NATIONS WILL DRAWN TO THE GLORY OF ISRAEL:** *"And the Gentiles shall see thy righteousness, and all kings thy glory: and thou shalt be called by a new name, which the mouth of the LORD shall name. Thou shalt also be a crown of glory in the hand of the LORD and a royal diadem in the hand of thy God. Thou shalt no more be termed be called Hephzibah-bah, and thy land Beulah: for the LORD delighteth in thee and thy land shall be married."*

APPENDIX IV

QUICK REFERENCES AND PROPHECIES

Messianic Prophecy #1: Messiah born as the seed of the woman (Genesis 3:15). (Known by Christian theologians as the Proto-Evangelium). Fulfilled in the New Testament by the birth of Jesus "born of the Virgin Mary under the Mosaic Law" (Matthew 1:18; Gal. 4:4-5). The crushing of Satan in mortal defeat was done by Jesus on the cross and will be shortly executed at His second coming (Romans 16:20).

- Targum of Jonathan (composed during the late 1st century or early 2nd century)
- Midrash Rabbah 23 (400-600 AD) from Rabbi Tanchuma
- Midrash Pesikita Rabbah 3:6 (400-600AD)

Messianic Prophecy #2: The Messiah, and King will come from the Tribe of Judah (Genesis 49:10) Fulfilled in the New Testament by Jesus Who was descended from the tribe of Judah. (Matthew 1:2, Luke 3:33, Hebrews 1:8-9, 7:14, Revelation 5:5).

- Targum of Onkelos (35-120AD)
- Targum of Jerusalem (late first century)
- Babylonian Talmud (200-500 AD)
- Sanhedrin Tractate 98b[3], *"What was the name of the Messiah...His name is Shiloh."* Midrash Rabah 97-99

Messianic Prophecy #3: A star will arise in the Sky to announce the coming of Messiah (Num. 24:17). Fulfilled in the New Testament with the birth of Jesus. Wise men from the east and the people of Judea saw the advent of a new star concurrent with the birth and infancy of Jesus the Messiah (Matthew 2:2,9).

- Targum of Jerusalem. Targum Onkelos

- Midrash Pesikta Sortarta, *"The week in which the Messiah will be born, there will be a bright __star__ in the east, which is __the Star of the Messiah__."*
- Midrash Devarim (Deuteronomy) Rabbah

From the Prophets:

Messianic Prophecy #4: Messiah shall come from the stem of Jesse (Isaiah 11:1-2). Fulfilled in the New Testament. Jesus was descended from the line of Jesse, King David's father (Matthew 1:6; Luke 3:32, Acts 13:22-23; Romans 15:1-2). Babylonian Talmud, Sanhedrin Tractate 93b[1]—Six descendants who would be a great blessing, David, is one of them, from the line of Jesse through whom Messiah would come—the greatest blessing of all.

- Targum Jonathan: *"And there shall go forth a King from the sons of Jesse, and the Messiah shall be anointed from his children's children."*
- Citation from *The Jewish Encyclopedia*, Volume 8: page 506, c. 1

Messianic Prophecy #5: Messiah will be a descendant (son) of King David (Jeremiah 23:5-6) Fulfilled in the New Testament. Jesus was born from the lineage of David, and hence called by the Messianic title, Son of David (Matthew 1:6, 21:9; Luke 3:31, Acts 13:23, Romans 1:3).

- Targum of Jonathan
- Babylonian Talmud, Tractate Babba Bathra 75b— One of the three names for the Holy One (the God of Israel) is Messiah the righteous, as it is written, "And this is His name whereby He shall be called, *"The Lord our righteousness"* (Jeremiah 23:6). Midrash on Lamentations 1:6

Messianic Prophecy #6: Messiah will suffer and be despised and rejected of men (Isaiah 52:13-53:12). Fulfilled in the New Testament when Jesus was despised and rejected by Israel (Mark. 8:31, Luke 17:24-25, Matthew 26-27, John. 18-19).

- Targum of Jonathan. Rabbi Mosheh El-Sheikhof (16th Century Rabbi of Safed, Israel) who wrote commentaries on the Earlier Prophets.
- Regarding Yesha'yahu 53 in the Tanakh, this rabbi wrote: *"I may remark then, that our Rabbis with one voice accept and affirm the opinion that the prophet is speaking of the King Messiah, and we ourselves shall adhere to the same view."*
- Up until the 19th century the majority of the rabbis, for the last 1,900 years, believed and taught Isaiah 52:13-53:12 which speaks of the suffering Messiah.
- Rashi the famous rabbi of the 11th Century (1040-1105) claimed the passage in question was speaking about Israel only. His peers and the rabbis who came after him soundly rejected this erroneous interpretation on grammatical and exegetical grounds.

Messianic Prophecy #7: Messiah to be born in Bethlehem (Micah 5:2). Fulfilled in the New Testament with the birth of Jesus the Messiah in Bethlehem (Matthew 2:1-5, Luke 2:4-11, John 7:42).

- Targum of Jonathan. Rabbi David Kimchi (1160-1235)
- Jerusalem Talmud (400-500 A.D) Tractate Berakoth 5a— *"The King Messiah... from where does he come forth? From **the royal city of Bethlehem** in Judah."*

Messianic Prophecy #8: Messiah will come as the King riding on a donkey (Zechariah 9:9). Fulfilled in the New Testament on Palm Sunday as Jesus rode into Jerusalem on a donkey (Matthew 21:1-9, John 12:12-17).

- Babylonian Talmud, Tractate Sanhedrin 98— *"Rabbi Joseph the son of Levi objects that it is written in one place, "Behold one like the son of man comes with the clouds of heaven," but in another place, it is written, "lowly and riding upon a donkey." The solution is. If they (Israel) is righteous, He shall come with the clouds of heaven, but if they are not righteous He shall come lowly riding upon a donkey."*

- Babylonian Talmud, Tractate Sanhedrin 99—Messiah will come riding on a donkey when the second temple is standing!
- Midrash Koehler, Rabbah 1:9, "Like the first redeemer so is the last redeemer. Just as it is said of the first redeemer, and Moses took his wife and sons and put them on a donkey (Exodus 4:20), so it is said of the last redeemer, *'Gentle and riding on a donkey.'*"

Messianic Prophecy #9: Messiah will be the Son of God (Psalm 2:7-12). Fulfilled by Jesus in the New Testament (Matthew 1:21-22, Mk. 14:61-62, John 1:34, Acts 9:20, 13:32-33, Hebrews 1:5, 5:5).

- Targum of Jonathan, *"The Kings of the earth stand up, and the Rulers are united together to rebel before the Lord, and to contend against **His Messiah**."*
- Babylonian Talmud, Tractate Sukkah. Rashi, *"Our rabbis expound it (Psalm 2) as relating to King Messiah."*

Messianic Prophecy #10: Messiah Will Be exalted at the right hand of God. Fulfilled in the New Testament when Jesus ascended to heaven to sit at the right hand of God the Father (Acts 1:9, 2:34-36, 7:55-56, Eph. 1:20).

- Midrash Tehillim in Psalm 2
- Midrash on Psalm 18:35

Messianic Prophecy #11: Messiah will appear before the destruction of the Second Temple (Daniel 9:24-26, Malachi 3:1). Fulfilled by Jesus with His triumphal entry into Jerusalem on Palm Sunday (Luke 19:41-46).

- Tractate Megillah (Part of the Mishnah)
- Rabbi Moses Abraham Levi (12th century Talmudist)
- Maimonides (Famous 12th century rabbi and author of the 13 articles of faith for Judaism)

REFERENCES CITED

[i] i. Martin Gilbert, *The Atlas of Jewish History*/William Morrow and Company, Inc. New York. 1969

[ii] Abram Leon Sachar, *A History of the Jews (Fifth Edition)* (New York: Alfred A. Knopf, 1967,) 251

[iii] Louis Harap. *The Image of the Jew in American Literature,* The Jewish Publication Society, 1974

[iv] Ibid

[v] Louis Harap. *The Image of the Jew in American Literature,* The Jewish Publication Society, 1974

[vi] John 18:10; Luke22:49-52

[vii] John 6:38; 16:28

[viii] Matthew 1:1-17, Jeremiah 23:5; 33:15 Isaiah 11:2-5

[ix] Revelation 19

[x] Postmodernism articulates that the world is in a state of perpetual incompleteness and permanent un-resolve. Postmodernism promotes the notion of radical pluralism that there are many ways of knowing, truths. From a postmodern perspective knowledge is articulated from perspectives, with all its uncertainties, complexity and paradox.

[xi] 2 Sam. 22:28

[xii] Jew is capitalized and gentile is not because gentile is a generic and general term that refers to nation groups; Jew speaks of one specific people group, and therefore it is capitalized.

[xiii] *Ovadiah*–Obad. 1:18

[xiv] Exodus 20:4

[xv] Acts 9:1-19; retold in Acts 22:6-21 and Acts 26:12-18.

[xvi] Lest you be wise in your own conceits, I want you to understand this mystery, brothers: a partial hardening has come upon Israel, until the fullness of the Gentiles has come in. And in this way all Israel will be saved. (Romans 11.25-26 ESV)

[xvii] Isaiah 11:1-9; Jeremiah 23:5-6, 30:7-10, 33:14-16; Ezekiel 34:11-31, 37:21-28; Hosea 3:4-5; Genesis 49:10, Isaiah 11:1, Jeremiah 23:5, 33:17; Ezekiel 34:23-24.

[xviii] Isaiah 2:1-4, 32:15-18, 60:15-18; Zep. 3:9; Hosea 2:20-22; Amos 9:13-15; Micah 4:1-4; Zechariah 8:23, 14:9; Jeremiah 31:33-34.

[xix] Hab. 2:14

[xx] Micah 5:2; Isaiah 2:3

[xxi] Luke 19:17

[xxii] 1Thes. 4:13-18; 1 Corinthians 15:21-23,51-53; Revelation 20:4

[xxiii] Revelation 20:4-6

[xxiv] Deuteronomy 28:13

[xxv] Romans 8:22

[xxvi] Daniel 2:44; 7:13-14,27.

[xxvii] Isaiah 11:1-2

[xxviii] I Corinthians 15:24

[xxix] 2 Ptr 1:16-18; Deuteronomy 27:12-13

[xxx] Zechariah 2:8

[xxxi] Deuteronomy 7:6; Psalm 135:4; Amos 3:1-2; Romans 11:1-2

[xxxii] Revelation 11:15, 21

[xxxiii] Deuteronomy 7:6-7; Jeremiah 30:17.

[xxxiv] Revelation 11:15, 21

[xxxiv] Deuteronomy 7:6-7; Jeremiah 30:17.

[xxxv] Zechariah 2:8; 12:10; Deuteronomy 32:10; Romans 11:29; Mat. 8:18; 19:28; 23:37-39; Daniel 12:9-13; Isaiah 1:26; Ezekiel 45:8; Hosea 5:15
[xxxvi] Isaiah 60:1; 20, 52:1
[xxxvii] Isaiah 11:12; 14:1-2
[xxxviii] Deuteronomy 5:1-3; Ezekiel 16:8, 43; 60-63; 15-34; Jeremiah 3:6-10; 31:1-5, 32; Hosea 2:2-5; 6-13; Isaiah 50:1; 54:1-8; 62:4-5
[xxxix] Ezekiel 16:8; 16:35-43; Hosea 2-5; 14:23; Isaiah 50:1,54; Jeremiah 3:6-10;
[xl] Genesis 12:1-3; Matthew 1:16; John 7:42; Psalm 132:11; 2 Sam. 7; Jeremiah 23:5-6
[xli] Zechariah 12:10; Hosea 5:15; Jeremiah 11:13
[xlii] Isaiah 35:3-10; 59:20; 65:21-23;
[xliii] Isaiah 32
[xliv] Revelation 22:2
[xlv] Zechariah 14:4
[xlvi] Matthew 25:31–46
[xlvii] Joel 3:2-12
[xlviii] Matthew 19:28
[xlix] Matthew 25:31–46

Metro Jewish Resources of the Assembly of God
Po Box 3777, Wayne, NJ 0747
973-461-9786

District Offices

National Office
1445 N. Boonville Avenue, Springfield, MO, 65802
417-8632-2781

New Jersey
2005 Columbus Road, Burlington, NJ, 08016
609-747-7878

New York Office
8130 Oswego Road, Liverpool, NY, 13090
315-622-2700

Spanish Eastern District
213 Old Tappan Road #1, Old Tappan, NJ, 07675
201-358-8610

Penndel
465 Westport Drive, Mechanicsburg, PA, 17055
717-795-5921

[1] Jeremiah 30:7
[1] 1 Corinthians 15:53, 1 Pet. 1:23.

BLANK PAGE FOR NOTES

BLANK PAGE FOR NOTES

BLANK PAGE FOR NOTES

BLANK PAGE FOR NOTES

-product-compliance